101 Ways
to Make Money
in the Trading-Card Market

101 Ways
to Make Money
in the Trading-Card Market

Paul Green and Kit Kiefer

Bonus Books, Inc., Chicago

98 97 96 95 94   5 4 3 2 1

Library of Congress Catalog Card Number: 93-74135

International Standard Book Number: 1-56625-002-1

Bonus Books, Inc.
160 East Illinois Street
Chicago, Illinois 60611

Printed in the United States of America

Cover cards courtesy of Paul M. Green:
Shaquille O'Neal (Fleer Corp.)
Troy Aikman (Pro Set Inc.)
Eric Lindros (Score)
Leon (Goose) Goslin (Goudey Gum Co.)

Books, like almost everything else, are not always fun. This one has been a joy in large part because someone around me was such a joy. That's why this book is dedicated to Teri who deserves a lot more than a book dedication but who is so understanding she'll probably be happy with it anyway. Teri, you're special and doing this book with you around was special too. Thanks.

All My Love,
Paul

Acknowledgements

Books aren't written in vacuums, and it's a good thing. Otherwise the houses of writers would be dirtier than they are now. What I mean is, every good writer needs a little help getting his writing done. In my case, I just opened up whatever books were on my shelf and started copying, and let me tell you, it was a great help. That accounts for the equal measures of Dave Barry, Ernie Pyle, James Thurber and Jeff Kurowski (editor of the *SCD Baseball Card Price Guide*) on the pages that follow. What it doesn't account for and doesn't show is the help and support of the people who really did make this book possible. That starts with my dear wife, Ann, who had her understanding stretched and her patience tested through the spring and summer, and goes on from there: to my parents, who got me into this mess by buying me cards until my ears bled and making me eat my vegetables; to my brother, Mr. Near Mint, who always came over to my room to look at my cards so he wouldn't get his own messed up; to Dean Listle, Darren Lee and Hal Hintze, the boys of Professional Hobby Consultants; to Hal again, for proofreading my copy and setting up at shows with me and other miscellaneous endeavors; to Jim McLauchlin, the official supplier of Puck bars to Paul and Kit's book, who convinced Fleer to pay him to go to Cooperstown; to Guy Wolcott and the helpful boys at AbleSoft (buy the software; it's great—even if you don't get it for free); to Don Butler, Jeff Kurowski, and Shawn Reilly at Krause Publications (oops!! They're all gone now); to Steve Ellingboe, Scott Kelnhofer, Tom Hultman, Mark Larson, Rick Hines, and Greg Ambrosius at Krause Publications (they're not); to Tol Broome, Bill Ballew, Jim Callis, Alec McAree, Dana Jennings, C.B. DeBennett, John B. Seals, and the rest of the nationwide network of true believers; to Paul, the best damn writing partner any hack could ask for; and all the people I've left out because if I've left them out they must have done something right.

Many thanks also to you for buying the book. Hope you enjoy it.

Kit Kiefer, Plover, Wisconsin

Writing anything with Kit is a little like shooting the rapids without a paddle. You're not quite sure where you're going, but you're certain it will be something you'll remember. As always, it's been fun and exciting, so he deserves special thanks.

A lot went on while I was writing this book. Some have suggested that the events were probably a book or a movie or both. Without reliving the best and worst times of my life, I have to give a special thanks to Tom Walker, who did his job and took a lot of unfair abuse for it. Teri and I will always be in your debt for your help, and Key West should feel the same way for your dedication to your job.

Sam, since we messed up your vacation you also deserve something, but, knowing you, it wouldn't be enough, so why bother.

Ken LaVoie, in addition to being a friend and landlord, helped in many ways, whether it was shopping, clean-the pool or just about anything I needed—now about that garbage disposal!

To Bubba John, who kept the office open when I retired—thanks for the lobsters and the laughs.

Special thanks have to go to Suzanne and Doug Leps and a number of others who never seemed to doubt us for a moment at a time when doubting Tom, Teri and me seemed fashionable.

And a special thanks to Jim and everyone else at the Cafe des Artistes at 1007 Simonton Street in Key West, who provided us with the best food on the island.

Paul M. Green, Key West, Florida

Preface

Kermit the Frog was right, as far as he got: It's not easy being green. What's even harder is making green, when the investment medium of choice is trading cards. Times have changed in the card market. Gone are the days, as Tennyson might have said, "When every morning brought a noble chance/To turn a case of Donruss at 100 percent profit." Now the prospective card buyer/collector/investor has to plan his buys and sells and have an overall profit strategy that goes beyond reading a few ads and buying the case of the week. What this book attempts to do is lay out a number of different tactics for buying and selling that you can combine to make your own personal card-buying and -selling strategy.

Like anyone who writes a book designed to help you make money, we make no claims to infallibility; we're encouraging you at some junctures to take risks that, like all risks, are far from sure things. On the other hand, we feel confident that if you follow our recommendations you'll do far better than the average card buyer, and what's more, you'll come out of it with an understanding of the card market, an appreciation of baseball cards, and the feeling that you really did enjoy yourself.

We certainly do enjoy ourselves. We've been involved in this business for more than a decade, and we think it's utterly screwy but delightful, like Carole Lombard with bubble gum. That's one of the reasons the tone of this book is lighthearted. We figured it was necessary. After all, these are trading cards we're talking about, and fun is one of the necessary components of trading cards. If it ain't for you, you might as well get yourself out of this market and into something like frozen pork bellies where you can really express yourself.

Speaking of expressing yourself, it's about time we started expressing ourselves. If you disagree with us, that's your prerogative. If you agree with us, you do so at your peril. And we think that's the way it ought to be.

101 Ways
to Make Money
in the Trading-Card Market

Sell all the cards you have right away.

Okay, so we're not subtle. We're not good-looking, either. But we don't pretend this business of card investing is more complex than it is, or more complicated than, say, making a can of frozen orange juice. Thaw the can (taking a nice hot shower with it is a favorite ploy), open the can, empty the contents into a pitcher, add three cans cold water, stir briskly. Same with baseball cards. With baseball cards, you're either thawed or you're frozen. Either you're in cards to make money or you're a collector. And there's nothing wrong with being a collector. Some of our best friends are collectors. But collectors do not expect to make money from their collections and do not make collecting decisions with the idea of making money. Of course, many collectors do make money in the course of buying and selling to fill their collections, but they consider it to be just something that happened, like thinking that was the brake pedal and not the accelerator. If you're a collector and want to continue being a collector yet want to make every collecting decision a moneymaker, go away. You can't have your orange juice in the shower with you and in the freezer at the same time. Making the decision to make money with cards does not mean you can't look at your cards, savor them, derive all the pleasure from them that collectors derive from their collection. It just means that you're honest with yourself about your motivations, and your primary motivations are financial.

Okay, big guy, now that you've come clean about What Men Really Want From Their Cards, what are you doing standing pat? Waiting for your kid to start college? One of the first rules in making money in cards is that you never just stand pat. Holding onto your cards and not selling them is a sure-fire way to make zero money—squat, zilch, diddly, nada—in cards. The only ways you make money in cards are by selling cards you have or by buying undervalued cards you don't have and selling them later on. Would you like a little more emphasis on that, just so you know it's important? Okay, here goes: *The only ways you make money in cards are by selling cards you have or by buying undervalued cards you don't have and selling them later on.* We have to chuckle every time we think of all the hundreds of thousands of card collectors out there, squirreling away their complete sets of late-'80s and '90s cards between the floorboards like they're sacks of gold dust, waiting for the day they can walk into the assay office, hand the boxes to the man and say, "I'd like full catalog value for these, please. And small bills." We have to chuckle a lot. In fact, we chuckle so much that the neighbors think we're a little barmy. But that's another story.

The next thing you have to acknowledge before you can start making money in cards is that you are not going to sell every card you own for the catalog value you think it merits. It never happens. And what's more, only a relative handful of people are going to want to buy your cards for any amount of money or equivalent merchandise at all. The pizza guy isn't going to be inclined to trade a pineapple-and-anchovy special for a Roberto Alomar, straight up. Beanie's Clutch and U-Joint isn't in the habit of taking '84 Donruss cases in exchange for viscous-coupling repair. And you cannot go into your card collection, pluck out a 1952 Topps Mickey McDermott, take it down to your local Tank 'N' Tummy and buy a six-pack of Master Cylinders and a copy of *Big Biker Mamas* with it. These are pictures of baseball players on cardboard, not pictures of presidents on U.S. legal tender. The sooner you acknowledge that the two are not necessarily interchangeable, the better—and the sooner we can get down to the business of getting you the maximum number of presidential portraits in exchange for your worthless pieces of cardboard.

And cards *are* worthless, when you get right down to it. You really ought to be thankful that anyone at all wants to buy the things. They have zero intrinsic value. The only value they have is the value that dealers, collectors and investors apply to them. And if any of these three groups attach what you think is an illogical value to a card you own or want to buy, you're sunk.

Listen, how do you think that an insert card of a mediocre player from an unpopular set—a ToppsBlackGold Brian Harper, for instance—gets to be worth what it is? Logic or convenience? Convenience, mostly. Internal logic and consistency. The number of people who want specifically a ToppsBlackGold Brian Harper card is small. The number of ToppsBlackGold completists is small. Once those two groups have their ToppsBlackGold Brian Harper cards, there are still plenty of cards left over for the people who want them. Sellers outnumber buyers because the demand for the insert product is short-lived and shallow. Prices plateau and fall back. And if you didn't realize this when you got your ToppsBlackGold Brian Harper card, you sure do realize this now.

But we're getting all ahead of ourselves, the insert card before the regular card, the Brian Harpers before the Mickey Mantles, the "i" before the "e" except after the "c". Let's get back to this business of you selling everything you have and running off and joining the Merchant Marine. You don't have to join the Merchant Marine; the Jaycees will do. But selling every blooming trading card you have and putting the money toward something tangible, like Homewrecker in the seventh race, makes sense. It's a simple thing to do, and this is a simple business. It's also a very active thing to do, as opposed to collecting. ("Collecting." Just the sound of it. It's so passive.) Cards, as we pointed out just a few paragraphs ago, have no intrinsic value. The number of collectors continues to shrink and the number of cards produced continues to grow. Upper Deck produced as many as half a million cases of baseball cards in 1992. Half a million cases of baseball cards translates to 4.32 billion baseball cards, or enough baseball cards for everyone in the country to get a couple of packs. And that's just Upper Deck, and just baseball. You can be excused if at times you think, "How can any modern card be worth any money if there are five million cards just like it floating around?" Good question! The answer is, "As long as you don't tell anyone there are five million cards just like your card out there, you're safe. But the moment you blab, look out."

We've established that it makes sense for you to sell every card you have right away; now to answer the question, "How?" Well, you can go about selling off your collection in a rational, orderly manner, or you can default to total panic mode and conduct one big baseball-card blow-it-out-the-bare-walls, everything-must-go sacrifice sale and be done with it. Take our word for it: Eventually you will panic. It's just too darn hard trying to get top dollar for every card. Fatigue sets in after a while.

Given that fact, we have a couple of recommendations for you. And given that this is a long book and we're going to be scuffling for sure-fire ways to make money in the trading card market RIGHT NOW towards the end, we're going to treat those recommendations as separate entities, though you and I know better. Ready? Swell! Here goes.

2 & 3

Know what you have.
Know what the other
guy has too.

Know what you have?" "That's an awfully passive, milquetoasty way to make money in the trading card market RIGHT NOW. You mean there's money to be made in just knowing what cards you have and what cards you need?"

You bet. Do you know what cards you have, what condition they're in and what they're worth? Do you know what you'd say if someone came up to you and offered you $10,000 for your entire collection? Would that be a good deal for you or a steal for him?

Has my point sunk in yet?

No? Well, how about if you walked up to a collector and offered him $5,000 on the spot for his entire collection? Did you take him for everything he was worth, or what?

By now you ought to have the idea: Information is money in this business. Knowing what you have and knowing its relative value is money.

Knowing what the other guy has and what its relative value is could be even more money. Even if catalog values aren't a reasonable yardstick of what you might expect to get for your cards, they're better than no yardstick at all. Know them, and incorporate them into an encyclopedic listing of your collection.

Encyclopedic listings don't have to take your entire lifetime to compile. You've got to save some time to be fruitful and multiply, after all. So get some card-collecting software to put on your computer—I have The Card Collector from AbleSoft (4824 George Washington Parkway, Suite 103, Yorktown, VA 23692), and I can't recommend it highly enough—and use that to speed the task of listing and valuing everything you have. Buy price guides and study the prices and the price trends. Don't look at the prices of cards that increase or decrease as being independent of one another; very often they're not. Most of the time it's not cards of individual players that go up or down in these guides; it's cards of entire classes of players—low-grade cards of Hall of Famers, '54 Topps commons, Brooklyn Dodgers, dead guys, whatever. Classes of cards go up in value because of blips on the demand scale. With almost any of the postwar cards listed in a price guide, supply is virtually constant; it's demand that changes, and demand that sets the price of cards. See what classes of cards are going up in value, see where the demand is, and see how that fits in with what you have—and with what the other guy has, too. That'll give you a sturdy foundation upon which to make your buying and selling decisions. And if you don't see the price trends heading in the direction of the cards you have, don't panic, but instead look for possibilities for you to capitalize on.

It all comes back to knowing what you have and studying what other people have and want. It really isn't that hard to do, and it really does pay off. And after all, how are you supposed to sell everything you have right now if you don't know what everything is?

Sell complete sets. And if you don't have complete sets to sell, get some.

This is a screwy business. Supposedly only true collectors collect complete sets. And supposedly the number of true collectors is on the decline. Yet one of the best ways for you to get top dollar for the cards that you sell is to sell those cards as parts of complete sets.

Blame the dealers for this one. Dealers want complete sets because they're less work for them and potentially more money. If the set doesn't have high-number scarcities and big dollar rookies and consists of uniformly high-grade cards, the dealer can sell the set as is. If the set has a lot of key cards, high-numbers or stars or big rookies, the dealer can break out these players, sell them for top dollar, and then sell the commons to a commons dealer, making a lot more money than he would if he sold the set intact. (Actually, you can do the same thing, but we can't discuss that under this heading.) Dealers want complete sets, and even though a set might be just a common or two away from completion, dealers will want no part of it. Incomplete sets mean work, and work subtracts from profit.

So avoid partial sets at all costs. If you have partial sets from your childhood or second childhood or third childhood or adulthood or puppyhood or whatever, spend the money it'll take to make those sets complete. The money you'll make on the other end will more than offset the money you'll lay out.

"But what"—I can hear you asking—"but what about those cards I have that are tiny fragments of sets, and sets that I could never afford to complete?" Simple: Don't complete those sets, silly. This is a way to make money in the trading card market RIGHT NOW, not an inviolable rule. If you know what you have, you know what you need. So compare what you need to what you have. Here's a good rule of thumb: If you sold everything you have from that set and still couldn't buy what you need to complete that set, you might as well give it up. If that's the case, sell the stars to a star dealer and sell the commons to a commons dealer, trade off whatever you can, or see if you can find someone who'll want to buy the lot. You're not exactly in a position of strength when you're working with an incomplete set, so the strategy is to get what you can, get out and keep moving.

Trading, that horrid word usually reserved for the last few holdout collectors who know no better, may actually be the best way for you to complete your partial sets or divest yourself of whatever sets you have that are too far gone to complete. Many people—like me—have no '55 Topps cards and would welcome a starter lot, provided someone does something with that one-third of a '64 set I have kicking around. Or maybe someone who has just the '66 commons you need to complete your set would like to get started with the '71 set but doesn't know where to start. We've seen these deals and lots of similar deals made at shows, and we've made similar deals ourselves. While they may lack some of the pizzazz of a standard sure-fire way to make money in the trading card market right now, they're good enough for us, thank you, and we wear good Republican cloth coats. We prefer to trade more recent cards for older cards whenever possible—lots of recent cards for just a few older cards, if that's what we have to do—and then take a more philosophical view: The numbers are in our favor. There are only a few thousand examples, if that, of this old common in this grade. There are millions of this recent star in this grade. We always prefer thousands over millions, except when it comes to people paying us money. Then we prefer millions. Tax-free.

Always buy the best quality you can afford. Always.

Does that sound like a Wal-Mart commercial? Sorry. We would never want you to conclude that buying cards is like shopping at Wal-Mart. There are no greeters at the door, for one thing, and it's hard to find really good circus peanuts at a card show. On the other hand, card stores and shows have all the boxes of Pro Line Portraits you could ever want, and Wal-Marts...well, they do, too.

Okay, so we're clear on the differences between buying cards and shopping at Wal-Mart. Let's talk about quality.

Quality cards sell better, faster and for proportionally more money than cards of lesser quality. Forget what the price guides have to say on this subject. Hang the price guides. We know what we see, and we do not see cards in Excellent condition selling for exactly one half of what cards in Near Mint sell for, and we most certainly do not see cards in Very Good selling for half of what the Excellent price would be if the cards in Excellent sold for half of Near Mint. It's a fallacy. And what's more, it's a fallacy that there are actually distinct grades like Excellent, Near Mint, or Very Good. Dealers bastardize them by cutting them into mid-grades like EX-NM and VG-EX, and then take things one step further by not pricing every Excellent or VG-EX card the same. You want the truth? There are no true grades. As one dealer in one of his few cogent moments told me, everything is a function of this one essential question: Is the card worth what the dealer is charging for it? When all's said and done, money is the grading scale in cards.

Okay, now that you've had one of the essential underpinnings of your faith in cards knocked out from under you, let's take a whack at another piling: The more expensive card is not always the better card to buy. Sometimes a high-priced card is poorly graded. Maybe the card has great eye appeal, sitting there in its inch-thick Lucite, but sometimes that inch-thick Lucite is hiding soft corners, creases, wax stains, or a counterfeit. So take every encased card you're thinking about buying out of it's plastic and look at it closely. Hold it widthwise up to a light and see what sort of surface gloss it really has. Check for centering. Make sure the print registration is right on. Examine the corners closely. Heck, you might even want to stick it under a 10X loupe and see what the dot pattern is like. If it's random, you might be looking at a counterfeit.

We're not going to engage in a discussion of grading standards and what constitutes what grade here. Buy a good catalog or price guide and they'll have the standards outlined in more detail than we'd ever care to go into. But once you're absolutely satisfied that this is the card you want, do one more thing: Comparison-shop. See what other examples of this card in similar grades are selling for. If you can't find the exact card, find comparables. Check their prices against what you think the price-guide ought to be, and then compare that to the card you're thinking of buying. See if the grade and price of this card are at least in the ballpark. And if they are, come back and ask yourself that key question: Is this card worth the asking price? If it is, and if it's absolutely the best-looking example of this card you feel you can afford, buy it.

We like top-grade cards so much we'll sometimes settle for a top-grade card of a lesser player over a lesser-grade card of a superstar, simply because we think the numbers are so slanted in our favor, and we're so sure we'll be able to find a buyer when the time comes to sell. But we have to be real firm about this; we do not do card dealers any favors. If a dealer has a card priced at a Near Mint price that we think is an EX-NM card, we walk away from it, plain and simple. We have our own standards for what constitutes a buyable card, and we adhere to them fanatically. We have to. If we don't, we don't make money. Simple as that.

Here's one of the reasons why. One favorite screw-the-customer ploy used by dealers involves the dealer telling the customer that the card the customer is selling is, say, Excellent, and then once the deal is done putting the card in the dealer showcase as a Near Mint card. It's bait-and-switch in reverse, and while not every dealer does it, it is widespread enough to make you not want to deal with any dealer ever.

(WHOA! Let me just stop right here to reassure all of you out there that we think most card dealers are fine, upstanding folks, friends and neighbors, and that we're sure they would never dream of buying a card at a lower grade and selling it at a higher grade. In fact, you can ask that dealer over there if that isn't so. And while you're at it, ask him for your wallet back.)

The only way you can protect yourself against dealer scams like the one we just described is to eliminate arguments. Buy the best grade possible. Buy perfect cards. Do you have any idea how small the universe of cards is? When one of the co-authors—the skinny one with the jaw—was editing *Baseball Cards* magazine, he received a question that went something like: "What percentage of 1956 Topps cards are in existence today?" He answered that only about 20 percent of the press run has survived,

JIM BROWN
CLEVELAND BROWNS   FULLBACK

with only about 7 percent of that 20 percent surviving in Near Mint or better condition. Figure that a couple hundred thousand cards of each player were printed—let's say 500,000 and err on the side of liberalism for a change. Of that 500,000, 10,000 cards survived. And of that 10,000, 700 survived in Near Mint or better grades. Seven hundred. That's all. And if one of those cards should get dropped accidentally, or creased, or waterstained, or you name it, then that's one more card taken away from that 700, one less card that can meet an ever-expanding demand for these cards. No wonder we say numbers are in the favor of older cards. No wonder we advise people to buy the best grades they can afford.

We realize we're sounding like our

STAR 84

ABDUL-JABBAR
NBA Scoring Leader

mothers now, and we apologize. We just feel that sometimes the only way we can get you to do something around here is to harp on it and harp on it and harp on it. And would you close that door? Do you want people to think you were born in a barn?

Buy cards of Hall of Famers.

Now here's a piece of advice that's truly generic: Buy cards of Hall of Famers. That's akin to telling the coin collector, "Uh, buy old coins," or telling the guy who plays the stock market, "Now, you'll want to buy only those stocks that go up in value." A good 90 percent of the buying and selling that goes on in the card and collectibles market involves the stuff of players who are in the Hall of Fame, ought to be in the Hall of Fame, or might someday be in the Hall of Fame. Given that fact, you'll probably be spending a good deal of your time dealing with Hall of Famers too. So you had darn well better know who and what you're dealing with.

First of all, another obviousity: Not all Hall of Famers are created equal. Babe Ruth and Lou Gehrig are on top and Hoyt Wilhelm is on the bottom. You'll pay less for Hoyt Wilhelm memorabilia but you'll sell it for less, too. Buying stuff of, say, Phil Niekro, figuring you'll double your money on the stuff when and if he gets elected to the Hall of Fame, is a sure way not to double your money. You want to strike a balance between affordability and obscurity, relatively speaking. You don't want to buy cheap stuff of Hall of Famers; you want to buy undervalued stuff. And there is a difference.

For instance, you can spend about $8 and get a complete 165-card Conlon Collection Babe Ruth set. It's a beautiful set of cards, very well done, and if you like Babe Ruth at all you ought to buy it. But it's not going to go up in value for many, many years, if then. On the other hand, you can spend four times that and get a 1961 Fleer Baseball Greats Babe Ruth in Excellent condition. The card is from a set that was issued after Ruth's death and it's not an attractive card by any means, but it's a scarcer card from an older set, a set where there is already an established level of demand, and a set that will probably go up in value over the next five years. You can buy that Babe Ruth card, enjoy it, and know you stand at least a fighting chance of selling the card for half again as much as you paid for it after five years. That's all you could hope for from any card.

As another, more versatile example, consider the 1964 Topps Giants set. It's an attractive set of cards; it really is. The 60 cards in the set are oversized, the photos are crystal-clear and the player selection is all you could wish for. From the standpoint of pure eye appeal, it's a much better set than the regular '64 set without all of the big set's dross. But the regular '64 Topps set sells for $3,000 and the Topps Giants sell for $110.

There's no reason at all why the Mantle card from the Topps Giants is an $18 card while the regular Mantle is a $250 item. Or why Sandy Koufax is $90 in the regular set and $18 (and a short-printed $18 at that) in the Giants. Or why Roberto Clemente goes for $110 in the regular set and $5 in the Giants. Long ago the '64 Topps Giants set got the undeserved reputation of being...well, not overproduced, really. Just undesirable, for whatever reason. And that black cloud continues to hang over the set, bringing down its value when all logic suggests it ought to be worth more.

But we're getting all ahead of ourselves again; we hate it when we do that. How to buy the right cards of Hall of Famers is a topic that could take up several chapters, and will. But just as a rule of thumb, remember: Buy smart. Don't buy cheap.

Buy Ted Williams cards.

Here's another one that might have you shaking your head. The Splendid Splinter wasn't on that many cards throughout his career, and the cards he did appear on come very dear indeed. The 1939 Play Ball Ted Williams could set you back as much as $2,000 for a nice example. The 1948 Leaf Williams is $900 in Near Mint—more like $1,500, if you can find a true Near Mint copy. His early Bowmans are legitimate thousand-dollar cards. Even one of his few Topps cards goes for no less than a couple hundred dollars. If you want to assemble a proper Ted Williams card collection you're looking at spending well into the mid-five figures.

On the other hand, you could buy smart and gobble up some Ted Williams cards that are no less scarce but simply a little less appreciated, The 1959 Ted Williams set is a perfect example of overkill. After more than a decade when Ted Williams cards were as scarce as hen's teeth—scarcer, if you knew some of the hens we do—an entire set devoted to Ted Williams sent collectors into sensory overload. The set was somewhat overproduced and did not sell well as a result (was it a Fleer product? You bet), and even today commons are priced at $5 each. That's probably a little too low to be real, but $7.50 apiece for nice commons isn't, and $7.50 each for cards of any player from 1959, much less cards of Ted Williams, is cheap. There is no reason not to make some Fleer Ted Williams cards a part of your Hall of Fame portfolio.

And while you're at it, score some cards of Ted Williams the manager. For the Senators' last three seasons in Washington Ted Williams was their manager, charged with the task of molding the Senators' collection of weak arms and weaker bats in his image. If you can imagine Ted trying to teach Tim Cullen and Brant Alyea how to find a pitch in their zone and drive it, you have some idea how tough it was for Teddy blankety-blank Ballgame of the Major blankety-blank Leagues. Williams's clubs won more games than they would have otherwise, but not nearly enough to matter. Williams appeared on manager cards in the Topps sets of 1969-72. Their values in Near Mint are $10, $7, $5 and $6, and the only reason the '69 card is $10 is because it's almost the last card in the set. There's a "Ted Shows How" card in the 1969 set that shows Williams with Mike Epstein and sells for about $3.25 in Near Mint—and it's a high-number, too. That's about $30 and change for five Ted Williams cards—and remember, Ted Williams was not exactly a frequent face in '50s sets, and $30 couldn't get you a Ted Williams card from the '50s in Kleenex grade. This is what we like to call a "value inequality," and we firmly believe that all value inequalities are reconciled over time.

One point of this little exercise is to get you buying Ted Williams cards. Williams is in all likelihood the greatest hitter who ever played the game, and any cards of him you can pick up are worth picking, even the new stuff from the Ted Williams Card Co. (We do admit to being a bit biased in favor of the Ted Williams Card Co., seeing as the words on the back of each card are not Ted's words but ours, but we won't be put out if you exercise your own judgment on this one.) Another point is to remind you that no player can be written off as being out of your league pricewise. There is always a way to get a desirable card of a big-name player if you're resourceful enough and know where to look. And this book is about nothing so much as it is about getting you to be resourceful and telling you where to look. And with that, let us bring up another name.

Buy Red Schoendienst cards.

Now, Red Schoendienst will never be confused with Ted Williams. Williams was a better hitter and Schoendienst was a better manager. But few Hall of Famers who played and managed were better at both than Schoendienst. As a second baseman Schoendienst had occasional power and the ability to hit for average, and as a manager Schoendienst led the Cardinals to two World Series and one World Championship.

Cards of Schoendienst the player are priced in with the other low-echelon Hall of Famers—Hoyt Wilhelm, Early Wynn, Enos Slaughter, Bob Lemon, Luis Aparicio. Fifteen or 20 dollars will get you most of them. But according to the price guides, cards of Schoendienst the manager are supposed to be priced with the commons, and so very often they get tossed in the cutout bin. The cards aren't commons, though; Schoendienst was a Hall of Famer who got into the Hall in part because of his abilities as a manager, and he didn't make all that many appearances on cards when he was a player. Did Schoendienst cease to be a Hall of Famer when he became a manager? Not really—only according to the baseball-card-pricing fraternity.

Well, don't believe them. Pick up some nice manager cards of Red Schoendienst at some very nice prices. Heck, you can even afford the better grades with these. If you can swing $15 for a card, pick up the Schoendienst card from the 1967 Topps set. It's a high-number, and a scarce high-number at that, and consider this: It costs as much as a Fred Talbot card from the same number series. If you can't afford Near Mint, a card in Excellent is only $7.50, and that's a buy, too. Otherwise, Schoendienst cards from the era tend to hang in the $1-$2.50 range in Near Mint when the Redhead is in a decent number series, which he usually is. Sparky Anderson cards are as much; so are cards of Hall of Famers like Hoyt Wilhelm and Jim Hunter in Excellent. Tony Conigliaro and Denny McLain cards are more.

While we don't want to make a blanket recommendation of manager cards, we would like to say that Walt Alston cards are cheap, Earl Weaver cards are cheap, Sparky Anderson cards are relatively cheap and Whitey Herzog cards might be a little bit cheap. Cards of all these managers ought to be worked into your investment portfolio when you have the opportunity. But Williams and Schoendienst should be your first two buys.

9

Buy mid-grade '50s and '60s cards of Hall of Famers.

Lots of average card buyers must get their hearts stuck in their throats when they contemplate buying top-grade cards of the players they idolized growing up: Mickey Mantle, Willie Mays, Duke Snider, Frank and Brooks Robinson, Bob Gibson, Sandy Koufax, Hank Aaron, Ernie Banks, Carl Yastrzemski. They're just so darn expensive. A '59 Topps Mantle is $400 in top grade; a Near Mint Snider from that same set is $400. A Near Mint '59 Koufax is $150, Mays is $150, Aaron is $125, Frank and Brooks Robinson are $150 each, and Bob Gibson is a whopping $400. (Okay, so it's his rookie card.) And the further back in time or the further up in series you go, the more expensive the cards get. Who can afford $225 for a '67 Brooks Robinson? Buying a few of these cards in top grade is fine; actually, it's highly recommended. But after a while you will get to a point where you say to yourself, "Okay, so what's more important: Buying a drop-dead-Mint '90 Leaf Frank Thomas or buying a VG-EX '56 Topps Jackie Robinson? The answer is: There's room for both (among all current players, Thomas is the guy who seems to have the most room for growth), but the numbers favor the Robinson card and so does the heart, and you do not get a lot of opportunities in this business to make both your heart and the cold, cold numbers out there happy at the same time.

About the only player who will give you a bit of trouble with affordability in lower grades is Mickey Mantle. Mickey Mantle is in a class by himself, though as time goes on the reasons for that become increasingly irrelevant, and you're still looking at $100-$150 for a nice VG-EX Mantle card from the late '50s or early '60s. Everyone else—Mays, Clemente, the Robinsons, Spahn, Berra, Ford, Reese, Aaron, Kaline, Mathews, Yaz, even guys like Stan Musial and Ted Williams who didn't exactly clog up the checklists in the '50s—is affordable, and the cards of second-echelon Hall of Famers—Aparicio, Alston, Wynn, Slaughter, Wilhelm, Schoendienst—are so cheap it doesn't even take thinking to jump on them, and jump on them hard.

Four or five dollars will get you an EX card of any of the decent Hall of Famers who played through the '60s and '70s: Willie McCovey, Billy Williams, Frank Robinson, Hoyt Wilhelm, Al Kaline, Luis Aparicio, Joe Morgan, Jim Hunter, Harmon Killebrew, Jim Palmer, Juan Marichal, Walt Alston, Don Drysdale, Rollie Fingers, and even Brooks Robinson or Rod Carew in some cases. You spend a little more, you get a little better card of these players, or you step up to a pretty nice card of players like Tom Seaver, Carl Yastrzemski and Johnny Bench. Even Pete Rose, if you feel like gambling.

That same sort of money won't go quite as far through the '50s, but it will enable you to make some buys. Casey Stengel cards from the early '60s, for instance. Luis Aparicio cards. George Kell cards. Whitey Ford cards. Pee Wee Reese cards. Early Wynn and Enos Slaughter cards. Multi-player special cards: Braves Fence Busters, with Hank Aaron and Ed Mathews, Joe Adcock and Del Crandall; Dodgers Boss and Power, with Walter Alston and Duke Snider; Sluggers Supreme, with Ted Kluszewski and Ted Williams. Each one of these multi-player cards is from the 1958 Topps set and goes for about $15-$20 in Near Mint. Go up a year and you can get an NM card of Mathews and Aaron alone for $50. Drop down a grade and you've got a heck of a card for $10. And lots of people are doing it. This is the direction in which collecting and investing in older cards is going.

If you pefer to spend more money and make value judgments as you spend, consider this: A gorgeous Warren Spahn card from the 1955 Topps set—a 38-year-old card, with a known universe of extant examples down in the hundreds or low thousands—costs about as much as the 1989 Upper Deck rookie card of Ken Griffey Jr., admittedly a gorgeous card, but one example of as many as a million extant examples. Okay, smart shopper, you make the call: Which one's the better buy? If you prefer, you can get only a slightly less gorgeous Duke Snider card from the same set for that amount, or a Roy Campanella card in Excellent—a really nice card of Roy Campanella, the all-around great hitting catcher and tragic symbol, a card that you don't see very often and ought to treasure when you see, for about $75. Can you beat it? No way. Should you buy it? Most definitely.

We could go on and on, and since it's a rainy day and we have nothing better to do, we will. Seventy-five bucks each will get you 1959 Topps cards of Stan Musial and Sandy Koufax—guys who are revered by thousands and didn't appear on many cards through their careers—in Excellent. Cards in EX look great; only the most demanding collector could be disappointed in the combination of looks and price. An EX Yogi Berra from the same set is only $40, Spahnie is $25, Ernie Banks is $35 and Al Kaline, Frank Robinson or Brooks Robinson is $25. These are great cards at wonderful prices. How can you say no to them?

The rap on EX cards from the '50s and early '60s was that they were hard to sell. No longer. Now an attractive EX card of a solid Hall of Famer from that era flies out of dealer showcases—because it's affordable, because people who can't swing $150 for a Near Mint Stan Musial can afford $75 for an EX version. We've seen the same thing start to happen with cards of '60s and '70s Hall of Famers like Johnny Bench and Reggie Jackson. The mid-grades are where cards are actually being bought and sold. And if you're buying and selling cards, it's where you ought to be doing a lot of your buying and selling.

Set up and sell cards at shows.

Sometimes we think we're Dionne Warwick, and sometimes we think we're proselytizers for the cause of Collectors Setting Up At Shows. We don't for the lives of us know why more collectors don't set up at shows. Maybe they figure only registered dealers are allowed to set up at shows. Truth of the matter is, most dealers aren't registered as dealers or vendors or anything, except maybe drivers. Sure, there are tax things you have to take care of—you need a sales-tax permit, for one thing, because that one-half of a percent of a time the taxman comes to call at a show you'll be set up there—but the government was good enough to make the procedures for getting the forms as easy as filling out your regular income tax or learning computer science from a non-speaker of English, whichever is greater. (Enter amount here.)

You'll need to make sure that the show you want to set up at is right for you, so before you pay the show promoter his table fee, ask a few questions—or better yet, go to one of his shows. Most promoters are not one-shot honchos. They promote several shows over the course of a year, even as many as one or two a month. See the mix of dealers the promoter has at his show, where they come from, what they sell, and what prices they're asking for their material. Analyze the crowd in terms of quality and quantity. See if they look like the sort of folks who would buy what you have to sell. You're probably not going to sell a bulk lot of '57 Topps commons to a 12-year-old kid, and you're also probably not going to sell hand-collated Leaf sets to a Brooklyn Dodgers collector. When you find a show that looks to have the right mix of people and dealers (you're right: Most dealers are not people), ask the promoter when his next show will be and whether you can get a table. If you can, give him his fee, fill out his form, and get to work.

A friend of ours, another baseball-card writer—if you can believe it—named Tol Broome, is great at ticking off the things a collector should do in getting ready to do a show. He's way too organized and rational in his approach, so we won't repeat it here. Besides, if you've been following this book along and doing some of the things we recommend, you've already done the most important pre-show prep of all: You've determined what you have and what it's worth. That's the tough part. The remaining things you have to do—getting the stuff you want to sell together and determining a price for it all—are easy. And setting prices is a whole lot of fun.

When you set prices on your cards, it's your opportunity to get back at all the dealers who have chiseled and conned dollars out of your pockets over the years. Your revenge will not come in outchiseling them; no, that's not ethical, though it can be a bit of fun in the proper company. Your revenge will come in undercutting the heck out of them.

If you're a collector set up at a card show, undercutting dealers is the name of the game. They have overhead; they have to worry about raising money to buy more cards. All you have to worry about is selling off what you have and getting the heck out. Walk the floor early in the show; have a buddy watch the table. See what other dealers are asking for their cards, and if you have the same thing and can afford to, undercut them by 10 percent. Remember, you're just looking for a profit out of your cards, something more than what you paid for them, nothing obscene.

The great thing about being set up at a card show is that you can buy *and* trade. If all you want to do is get out, this isn't such a wonderful thing, but otherwise you have the chance to lap up some real nice bargains. Eighty percent of the time you'll be offered only very modern star cards, many just snatched from a pack minutes before they arrived at your table in some young entrepreneur's hands—scram, kid—but that other 20 percent of the time can be real interesting. If you can, trade your new stuff for his nice older stuff. If you can't work out a new-stuff-for-old-stuff trade, buy the old stuff and let the new stuff walk. Remember, when you're a dealer all buys and trades are supposed to work out in your favor. So take that 30 percent you need to cover overhead; build it into the buy or trade. If you really want the card, you can let your collector instincts take over eventually. But whenever you buy or trade at a show as a dealer you're working from a position of advantage—at last.

If you enjoy the time you spend as a dealer at one show, try selling at another show or two. Just don't get the idea in your noggin that this is a great way to make a living, because it isn't. It's a lousy way to make a living, and lots of people who used to own card shops can vouch for that. You want to be smart enough in this business to make money selling cards, but not so smart that you decide to open a shop. It's a tough trick to pull off, but if you can do it you'll be sitting pretty.

11

Recognize hype.

Hype simply sounds exciting. Like a barker in front of a New Orleans dance hall, hype is the use of words to make something seem a lot more exciting than it really is or, in the case of cards, a lot more valuable.

The sports-card market has more than its share of hype and, unfortunately, more than its share of people taken in by offers regularly promoted as too good to be true. If you can't learn to recognize and avoid offers that require hype to sell, you are going to lose money and probably a lot of it.

Perhaps the most frequent form of hype today comes in the form of "limited editions." Just what does that mean? The working assumption is that the production numbers are small, too small to meet the demand for them, thus assuring a profit for the owners. It's frequently not true, although it's always true that there is a profit for the manufacturers. That's why companies such as Topps and Fleer are worth millions of dollars and are listed on major stock exchanges while the memorial card collection of your average buyer is worth very little.

"Limited edition" is not exactly defined in the card market. It could mean limited to 10,000 cards of each player, which is most often still plenty for the demand. It could mean limited to a number adequate to provide one for every living thing west of the Mississippi. It could even mean limited to cards enough to stretch to Uranus and back. Without a working definition of the terms, limited edition is a trap to be avoided.

Even if we actually knew what a given limited edition was in real and trustworthy numbers, that would be no guarantee of financial success. It's not how many of a given item exist that alone determines value.

It's a sad fact of life that there are countless ugly items out there that are one-of-a-kind. My mother owns one particularly awful papier-maché bird Christmas ornament. It was made when I was in kindergarten. The beak has dropped off and the decades haven't been kind to that orange head or blue body. Plus, it always looked more like a spitball with sequins than a bird anyway. All that said, it's unique. Aside from being unique, though, it's valuable only to mother and me, and she doesn't have to bid on it, while to me its value is roughly what a burglar would charge to break into her house and destroy the blooming thing.

So you can limit something to one, ten, ten thousand, one million or any quantity you want, but it's not guaranteed to be valuable.

Sometimes the hype is so extreme as to make one question why anyone would be sucked into the deals in the first place. Take the notion of cards with prices that are ready to "explode". Now, someone seems to think that the prices will go significantly higher. But do you remember the Challenger? To NASA it may have been a major malfunction, but to everyone else the Challenger exploded. When it happened the spacecraft did not go higher, it fell down. Now if prices explode in that manner, it doesn't exactly mean they will go higher, does it?

Actually, come to think of it, maybe the notion of exploding prices isn't hype, but rather honesty about the future of the cards being offered. Either way, most collectors read "exploding prices" as "much, much higher prices," and that's hype.

The simple method for dealing with hype is just to avoid it. If something needs to be hyped to sell, that in itself tells you about all you need to know about the demand for it—and that spells trouble for price increases. So even though hype might make something sound good, don't buy the items. Their prices might explode more like the Challenger than like a Nolan Ryan rookie card.

12

Do the same as the advertisements.

How would the Home Shopping Network look in print? Check the weekly *Sports Collectors Digest* and you might very well get an idea. Not that *SCD* is huge; it's just like the St. Louis phone book—published every week. Is there that much news? Of course not. The weekly *SCD* amounts to a few articles, some press releases, pricing information and, oh yes, enough advertisements to make any home shopper happy for the rest of his life or wallet, whichever gives out first.

Some might think all those advertisements (probably a couple pounds' worth each month) are a waste of time, but nothing could be further from the truth. In fact (and we know our friends at *SCD* will love this), those pages should be required reading as the best guide to the baseball card market anywhere, bar none. Yes, better than Beckett, better than any column or book, better than any publication you could name. There is nothing better in timely information in the hobby than an SCD advertisement.

Does that mean you should do whatever the blaring headlines tell you to do? Heavens, no—that would be the worst possible thing you could do if you wanted to make money in the sports card market.

Think about it for a minute. Would some friendly dealer buy a full page in SCD to make you rich? Would anyone in his or her right mind spend hundreds of dollars to buy a page to get you to sell them cards because they were convinced the price would fall like a rock? Of course not.

The same applies to selling you cards. Many dealers might be fine people, considerate of others, friends to wildlife and serious about recycling, but do you really think that they are offering to sell you cards just so the value will go up and you'll make money? Consider some recent *SCD* advertisements that included offers touted as "Deal of the Decade," "Great Investment," "Great Buy," "Super Cheap," "Everyone who reads this ad should take advantage of a once-in-a-lifetime great deal," "HOT, HOT, HOT," or my favorite, "You Will Go Ballistic," whatever that means. Who could possibly think this sort of hype is part of a public-spirited effort on the part of dealers to get you to buy their cards so that you and not they can reap the profits of their once-in-a-lifetime offers?

The evidence is that most often you will be well advised to do what the dealers are doing, not what they say you should be doing. If they're selling Gretzky cards and offering to buy Mel Ott cards, then you should be doing the same thing. Happily, with their ads in *SCD* they make it very easy for you to know what they are doing, and more often than not they're right.

13

If it sounds great, it probably isn't.

There they are, the smiling hosts of your favorite shopping network. Okay, so some days their smiles are a little like what you might find on a hopping barracuda, but today they're friendly and they're offering you something very special: great deals on baseball cards, autographs or related items.

Or maybe it's not a shopping network but a commercial run on a network or major cable station. Hundreds of cards of your favorite team, sport or Indian tribe including "valuable rookie cards" for just under their catalog value. Of course, they never say which rookie cards are included or any of the other details which might actually convince someone the deal was worth anything like the $8.95-plus-shipping-and-handling price.

They don't tell you the details for a good reason. The catalog values on modern cards are wildly inflated about 98 percent of the time. The cards and shipping probably represent a profit of about 90 percent of the price, and they are cards with virtually no resale value.

Why otherwise thoughtful people sucker for such deals has always been one of life's little mysteries, like why some charcoal lighter works only on the metal part of the grill and not on the charcoal itself. There just is no explanation—except in the case of the TV offer, buyers feeling the deal sounds too good to be true plus the fact that it's on TV so it must be true, much like *Murphy Brown*.

Now, if you're tempted by TV offers, just remember *Murphy Brown* Isn't Real, and great TV offers almost always aren't either. Save your money for a pocket fisherman, get them to throw in some free carving knives, or just do some research and spend it on real card deals.

14

Give away price guides.

What's the book price?" Anyone who has ever attended a card show has heard that question. In fact, you've probably heard it even more than other more important questions such as "What's for dinner?"

People have been saying it for years, but it's worth remembering: Price guides price cards, but they neither buy nor sell them. If you think that's an insignificant point, try and sell a 1990 Leaf Bo Jackson for $4. Or try and get $1.75 for a 1975 Steven Rice Upper Deck Extended hockey card. It can work the other way as well. If you can buy a T214 common in VG, as one suggests, for $97, take it, because the only one offered in the past year had a minimum bid price of $500.

No, the price guides aren't trying to rip you off (remember, they don't buy and sell cards). They do, however, take months in production, and in that time Dikembe Mutombo can be eclipsed by Shaquille O'Neal, Troy Aikman can win the Super Bowl and Eric Lindros can lose Rookie of the Year. All those events change prices up and down, but the book can't change with events.

With modern card production, it's becoming impossible even to update prices each year in anything but the most superficial manner. That would be okay if you were buying cards with Monopoly money. The problem is your profits and losses are in real dollars.

Just look in catalogs. In many you'll find they use a formula. The Near Mint card is listed at one price. The Excellent condition example of the same card is 50 percent of the price of the Near Mint, while a Very Good example is 50 percent of the Excellent price. It's a neat system, and if you happen to have to price 350,000 cards it saves a lot of time, maybe even years of time. The problem is it's not accurate, as there are virtually no cards where the Excellent is worth 50 percent of the Near Mint price of the same card.

The simple truth is that you can make a lot of money buying some cards at book price and selling others at book price simply because the book is outdated or wrong. You can also lose a lot of money going by the book. Generally speaking, the ones who make money by the book are dealers and the ones who lose are investors.

The way to make money is to learn the market using price guides as guides to relative value. They can tell you that the Yzerman rookie card in the 1984-85 OPC set is worth more than the Gretzky card in that set, but the minute you use them to tell you that the Yzerman is worth $55, you would be well advised to throw the price guide into the nearest river.

15

Consider selling and holding costs.

It costs money to own cards, autographs, memorabilia, or anything else, for that matter. If you doubt it, try having a stuffed moose in your living room and figure out your rent or mortgage payments for the beast, and you'll find it's not cheap.

It also costs money to buy cards and related items. You start with the price of the card, then you add in shipping and handling costs, then additional costs such as 10 percent buyer's fees from auction. Then add in the interest you could be making on the money and the interest you are paying if you happened to borrow the money, and you'll find you've got a lot of small individual costs that become significant when taken together. Moreover, to sell the item (especially at auction) you get to pay many of the same costs again.

And it's not limited to the costs of buying and selling, as you have that storage thing to consider as well. In the case of many items such as cards it's not a big deal, but when cards become cases of cards the situation changes. In fact, there are many collectors and dealers who have ended up expanding into garages and even empty buildings just to find room for all the stuff. As you do, there are also little matters such as insurance, since things like floods and hurricanes are known to happen, and that can be costly, to say the least.

While some may think it's not a big deal, these items can easily require that your cards or other purchases increase in value by close to 50 percent the first year just for you to break even if you choose to sell.

16

Have a plan.

Don't just throw money at the problem. Someone with a love of sports and money in his or her pocket at a card show is a little like the proverbial kid in the candy store. He tends to want everything and, with good reason, the dealers are willing to oblige.

Even the best of us have weak moments. That autographed ball of our favorite team is just too good to resist; or that kid looked so good in the NCAAs, why not buy 100 of his rookies? The possibilities will end long after your bank account and sometimes you'd just swear the stuff is calling for you to take it home.

Heartless though it may be, ignore those cries from the homeless unopened packs, game-used bats and whatever else is calling your name. Have a plan for what you are buying and stick with the plan.

The best reason for a plan is that it will be formulated when you're at home, well out of the range of people offering you great deals and sure things. If you're collecting Hall of Fame basketball players, then you want a Paul Arizin card and not a hockey stick signed by the Ottawa Senators.

Moreover, if you concentrate on the items you're collecting you'll learn more about them and their rarity and accurate pricing as opposed to nifty tidbits about Beatles cards, which, while interesting, are not the place where you've invested your money. With relatively few books about cards available, every show is a precious opportunity to learn and shouldn't be wasted trying on replica jerseys.

There's another reason to have a buying plan, and it's one learned by many from sad experiences. The scenario is usually a limited budget and a deal you just can't pass up at the third table you visit out of 100 dealer tables at the show. Sure, you don't need a Joe Montana rookie, but at that price you just can't say no.

About 30 tables later comes the first rub. At that table you find the N172 card of Old Hoss Radbourn that you need for your Hall of Fame collection. You haven't seen one in eight months and you *had* the money, except now all you have is a Joe Montana rookie. You go home without the Radbourn.

Then comes the second rub. The Montana that was so cheap was inexpensive for a reason. It has a corner crease just barely visible under magnification, so the great deal wasn't so good after all. You end up losing money and waiting another year before you find another Radbourn, which of course is 25 percent more than the one you saw at the show.

This sort of thing happens all the time. If you had had a plan and stuck with it, there would have been no loss on Montana and you would have had your Radbourn. While impulse purchases can be fun, they are rarely money-makers. With all that temptation, few of us can resist making those expensive mistakes unless we have a plan and stick to it.

17

Buy hockey tobacco cards.

It's a little-known secret south of the border, but everyone in Canada knows that tobacco hockey cards are very tough and in great demand.

It seems that in the United States, where a lot of people still don't know the difference between Vezina and marigold, hockey tobacco cards are not well known. That is likely to change, and change dramatically, as hockey draws more fans and collectors who discover that back when they were making T206 Wagners, up in Canada they were making C55 Vezinas.

As a rule, they made a lot fewer C55 Vezinas or C56 Lalondes than T206 Cobbs or T205 Johnsons. Moreover, for some unknown reason the Vezinas, Lalondes and others have generally fared very poorly over the years in terms of their state of preservation. Perhaps Canadian youngsters in the early 1900s just liked to bend cards, as many C-cards found today tend to grade somewhere between Good and Very Good. Relatively few make it to Excellent and virtually none make even a loosely defined Near Mint.

Under the circumstances, any hockey tobacco card is a solid choice whatever its grade, but especially so in higher grades. One problem is that, assuming you can find any, you should expect to pay prices safely above current catalog values, as American catalogs are generally least accurate when it comes to hockey, and the older the hockey, the greater the problem.

You must remember that where early hockey cards are concerned, literally the entire supply comes from Canada, and free trade or not, our friends in Canada don't seem highly motivated to part with their treasures for the sort of prices American catalogs seem to think they are worth.

It is a little worrisome to pay well over catalog, but for hockey tobacco cards the worry is misplaced. They are about the bluest of blue chips. Sure, you buy them this year and your friends aren't likely to light sparklers and ring bells in your honor, but don't worry. Hockey is growing and hockey tobacco cards will have their day.

18

Sell autographs.

Supply and demand: It's all you ever need to know and it's the only standard you need to apply. When you do apply it to something like modern autographs, there is only one logical conclusion and that's to sell, to sell *now* and to stop buying.

Think about it for a minute. People stand in lines for hours waiting to pay good money to have a player or ex-player sign a picture. The process is time-consuming and expensive when you figure out you had to drive to the show, pay admission, drink an expensive Coke while waiting and then pay for the actual signature.

In the end, virtually everyone who wants a given player's signature gets it. The player then signs all the mail-order requests and leaves behind a trail of happy new autograph owners. But would they be so happy if they tried to sell their new treasures? Only if they got lucky and the player died on the way home. Now, is that a good system?

The problem with buying current autographs is a simple one. The average player can sign about 300 items an hour. Let's assume he does that a modest 300 days a year, which isn't all that much considering most do some signing every day. That comes to a total of 90,000 autographs of just one player every year. Now, if a 25-year-old star does that for the next 50 years before passing away at the not terribly old age of 75, that comes out to 4,500,000 signed items. At, say, $10 a pop, that's $45 million in one player alone. Are you getting the picture yet? There's no way, no how that there are 4.5 million people who want this character's autograph or $45 million to support the market in them, and in reality these numbers are probably conservative.

For a time a player's demand can keep up with his ability to crank out signatures, but not forever, not even for long. Moreover, once his career is over and he has fewer demands on his time, does anyone seriously think he's going to sit at home in retirement and limit himself to one hour of signing a day when someone is willing to pay money for this difficult job?

And how do we get the prices of today? Does the market actually support them? Again, for a time, maybe. It takes a while for every sucker to shell out his or her $250 or whatever for an autographed Mickey Mantle or Joe DiMaggio bat. This too shall pass as people realize there is no panic. Eventually, all the autographed pictures, bats, and whatever bits of clothing a player has signed will return to the market, and when they do, heaven help you if you're still holding on to such treasures.

There may be one or two exceptions as car accidents and the like take their toll, but there is not enough carnage on the highways, waterways and in the friendly skies to produce enough autographs that do well to compensate for all the price declines waiting to happen.

The way to approach the current autograph situation is to buy one if you can't get the player to sign for you. Buy it as you would almost anything else. Assume there is no profit potential and that way you won't be disappointed.

If, however, you are buying signatures on the notion that there is going to be some profit, sell them. Just cut your losses and forget about it because the numbers don't lie, and there is just no way to make them work in your favor.

19

Buy Turkey Reds.

They just don't make them much better than the big, beautiful cards known as Turkey Reds. Technically called T3s, the Turkey Reds really were premium issues for various types of tobacco. If you smoked enough, saved the coupons, and mailed them in, you got to choose one of the 100 baseball players or 25 boxers.

It seems easy enough, but put in the context of 1911, there were probably not a lot of parents willing to supply enough cigarette coupons for their children to put a serious dent in a Turkey Red collection even though the cards were attractive $5\frac{3}{4}$" x 8" pictures of the stars of the day.

The artwork on the Turkey Reds was in many cases an expanded version of what was used on T206s. That spells popularity because it's really the classic baseball card art from the early 1900s.

Today, Turkey Reds remain among the most popular of the early

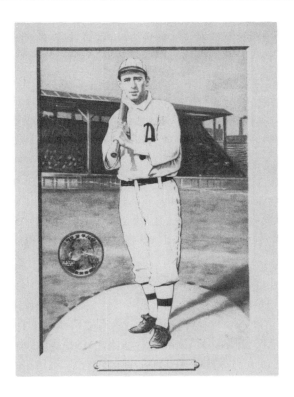

cards. They featured almost all of the big names of the early 1900s, but owing to the fact that they were premiums and not readily available in cigarette packs, they are much less common than their smaller T206 counterparts.

Not only were Turkey Reds comparatively rare, but they also suffered from use more than most cards. Their plain borders showed wear quickly and their size made them popular items to tack on a child's wall. Perhaps today that might not seem like much decoration, but after looking at a few Turkey Reds in top condition you might well reconsider.

There will always be plenty of demand for Turkey Reds, even though much higher prices could possibly keep them from advancing too quickly. It's just that Turkey Reds have almost everything you could want: rarity, beauty and big-name stars. In cards, it just doesn't get much better than that.

20

Sell black-and-whites.

It's not that hard to figure out. Why have a black-and-white television when color is available? While dealers who own large inventories will not like to hear it, black-and-white cards just do not sell.

Sure, there are a couple exceptions. Babe Ruth's rookie card is black-and-white. The classic Casey Stengel is a black-and-white, and there are Joe Jackson black-and-whites that sell although they don't bring the sort of money they might if they were in color.

If you take away those few exceptions, the situation gets real grim for black-and-whites. You can regularly find them for fractions of their "book" value and even then there are very few takers.

It's not as if the black-and-white issues are merely waiting to be discovered. They've been sitting around for years, and with the possible exception of N172s, which are really the main card set from before 1900, there has been no change. If anything, black-and-whites today are less popular than they were a few years ago and the trend is not a good one.

While the case can probably be made that black-and-whites are cheap, that there has to be some basic reason to expect an increase in demand as the supply is relatively stable, to date, there is no reason for such belief, and no logic for keeping any but the best black-and-whites in your collection.

21

Buy cheap old cards.

Sometimes the best way to make money is to minimize the amount you can lose. That may come as a bit of a shock to anyone who has just spent $30,000 on a Mickey Mantle card, but let's face it, is the Mantle a bigger risk than a low-grade $5 T206?

There are some limitations to this concept. Cards that are damaged or altered in any way are not a good risk: You are buying someone else's problems, and whether it's a bad car or a bad card, who needs it?

Besides, there are plenty of good, if not great, deals out there waiting to happen if you just shop around enough and get a little lucky.

First, forget the catalog. It will tell you that old cards such as T206s in Very Good condition sell for around $12 each or somewhere in that range. Well, maybe in a dealer's dreams, but on a regular basis on the wholesale level they don't bring anything like that. A few dollars each or maybe $5, but much cheaper than any catalog would have you believe.

The catalog doesn't mean to lead you astray, and there are probably people out there who have and will continue to pay book-level prices for VG T205s, but then there are people out there who honestly think you have to pay sticker price at an appliance store or that your odds of winning a few million in the lottery are actually better than your odds of being hit by lightning.

Yes, there is one born every minute, and it so happens that goodly numbers of them seem perfectly willing to pay too much for rather ordinary cards. Dealers love them, they make a living off them, they name their children after them, sing their praises around the Thanksgiving meal and remember them almost as fondly as they do people who buy unopened cases that have gone down in price.

All that said, forget the glory— don't be one of those people. Walk the aisles at a card show, look around, see the dealer with piles and piles of T206s or Goudeys or whatever. Even at prices close to legalized theft, the dealer has a lot of money invested in those piles and a lot of money invested in the hotel room or the dinner he hopes to buy the young lady two tables down. He needs the money, too, and even a little is better than nothing. It's also better than having to cart all of those cards back home and considering whether it was really such a good idea to leave that job at Midas.

If you make that dealer a fair offer you just may find that those $15 R206s can be had at $5 each because a $2 profit per card is better than not selling them at all.

Understanding that, you can make some good deals from time to time, and although you may not make a fortune you certainly run little risk of significant loss. Plus, it's a lot easier for a $5 card to go to $10 than it is for a $50,000 card to go to $100,000.

22

Consider whether superstars can improve.

It's nothing against Michael Jordan or anyone else who completely dominated a sport, but let's get realistic for a couple minutes.

Jordan was at the top of his game, not unlike the Wayne Gretzkys and Joe Montanas of recent years. Card prices for such superstars tend to follow fairly closely the progress of the career of the player.

No matter how great, no matter how dominant, somewhere along the line age will take its toll. The pressure, the physical poundings, but most of all the simple fact that, yes, even though it doesn't always seem like it, Michael Jordan and all others are still human.

Once the decline begins and once the greatness starts to fade ever so slightly, so too will demand for the cards. This does not mean sharp declines in price, but it does mean a softening in demand which at minimum spells a slowdown in price increase.

This does not mean that you

should necessarily unload all of your Michael Jordans, or any other superstar for that matter. They are still the blue chips of modern cards—if there are such things in the current age of high production.

On the other hand, you may want to sell or trade off some duplicates.

Remember, the real key to modern cards is buying something *before* everyone else wants it and then selling the item *when* everyone else wants it. Waiting too long to sell is one of the most, if not the most, common error made by investors and it's an error you can avoid if you only remember that no one puts a puck by, or dunks over, time.

23

Sell "W" cards.

Just calling them ugly doesn't really do them justice. They are a lot worse than that. Perhaps they were a bad third-grade art project in the 1920s. Had there been cardboard mercy killings at the time they would certainly have been at the head of the line. What are these abominations? They are politely known as "W" cards.

Issued in strips or individually, the "W" card is an unusually unattractive piece of low-quality paper generally featuring an artist's rendition of a star of the day that has about as much similarity to the player's actual appearance as a piece of lava rock has to a football. When such quality artwork wasn't available, bad photographs sufficed.

In fairness, there are a couple of artistic exceptions, but those pitiful numbers go a long way toward proving the point. One other point that could be made in favor of the "W" card is that the strips made for interesting combinations such as Ty Cobb and Babe Ruth together in a strip. Their only other significant plus is they are cheap.

Some who aren't aware of what they are getting are lured into "W" card purchases as a cheap way to get a Babe Ruth or Ty Cobb, but there is a reason why they are so cheap.

Remembering that supply and demand determine price, there must be either a very good supply of these little beauties or virtually no demand. The fact is that considering their age, both negatives apply.

The grim prospect for the "W" card and its owner is that neither the supply nor the demand is likely to change any time in the future.

The best that can be said of the "W" cards at this time is that you probably won't lose too much money on them—it would be hard to spend much on them even at inflated prices. If profit is the name of your game, then the "W" card is not your ticket. Try pork bellies, try swamp land, try the Brooklyn Bridge and try to sell your "W" cards before you start to delude yourself into thinking they aren't all that ugly.

24

Buy football.

You make money buying something when it's down in price. For whatever reason, people who buy cards seem to ignore that fact. The more something goes up in price, the more they seem to want it and that's not good for price appreciation.

Lately, things haven't been too good in the football-card market. Part of the problem may be the little matter of virtually everyone making football cards. And there is the fact that no one can put together a package that contains all possible rookies.

Prices are down, which has done nothing for interest based on the lemmings-to-the-sea nature of things in cards. Moreover, football, with Joe Montana hurt and aging, is suffering a superstar crisis. Troy Aikman may be a great quarterback, but he still isn't mentioned in the same breath as Michael Jordan or Wayne Gretzky.

It's not just the modern cards either. Football cards may not have the long history of hockey and baseball, but there are plenty of interesting and even rather tough cards from the 1950s that should be producing waves of astute collectors and investors. Instead, they are sitting in holders waiting to find anyone who cares.

It's not really a pretty picture, but then it's also typical of what markets go through from time to time. It's a perfect time to take a

JIM THORPE   *Halfback*

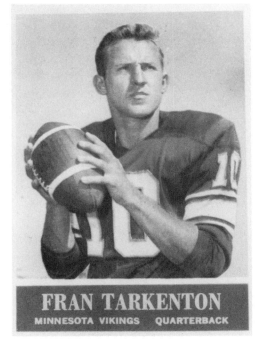

FRAN TARKENTON
MINNESOTA VIKINGS   QUARTERBACK

long hard look at football as things are likely to change and it makes sense to be in before people discover football rather than after they all wake up.

Good football investments abound. Start with the cards of the 1950s. For not much money you could be putting together sets or concentrating on high-grade Hall of Fame members. That pattern is available all the way to the 1980s.

There really is very little in the football market that seems overpriced at the moment. Joe Namath and some of the Packer greats from the Lombardi era might be a bit out of line, but otherwise there are very few danger signals and even these few can be mitigated by a stronger overall market.

25

Sell exhibits.

For about 50 years there has been a wide range of cardboard pictures of sports heroes that today can be considered cards. Exhibits are among them. They are included in the bigger catalogs and even have a few collectors.

Despite their recognition, exhibits have some negatives that make them marginal investments at best. The first of these is their size, which is basically that of a postcard. Although it should not disqualify them totally as having potential, it's a negative to some, and when you're talking supply and demand as price determinants, any lessening of demand has to hurt.

The second problem is that exhibits tend to feature absolutely nothing on the back. You just got them from machines and since you had already paid money for the card there was no reason to place advertising on the back. The makers also didn't see any reason to clutter up the emptiness with things like statistics, so you're talking about a postcard with a blank back.

Then we come to the pictures. Let's face it: Photography on cards wasn't always good, but with exhibits we're talking low budget all the way. In fact, for much of their period of production the best cards were color artwork and not photography, which at the time was something short of excellent.

In addition, exhibits are black-and-white. Although that's not a total disaster, it doesn't help either.

If you put all these factors together, while none by itself is enough to mean exhibits are to be avoided, the combination simply does not lend itself to a great following and that's the problem with exhibits. With a limited collector base and only the positive of low prices, exhibits are not likely to yield substantial returns any time soon.

26

Sell all the insert cards you have right away.

From time to time the people who make baseball cards call us up and ask our advice on this, that or the other thing. We always tell them to make a *Weekly World News* set and hope that will be that (can you just imagine a Titanic Baby Found Alive rookie card?), but from time to time they're not satisfied with that sage advice and press us.

"What else can we do?" they ask. "What can we do with our insert cards?"

"Throw 'em out," we say.

"Oh, we couldn't do that," they say, and then that really is that.

Cardmakers are hooked on insert cards. They have to be. With 95 percent of their sets that's the only way they have of selling the cards they make.

Think about it: Did 1992 Fleer baseball sell on its own merits, or because of the Rookie Sensations cards certain packs might have contained? Lest Fleer think we are picking on it and it alone, did Topps Beam Team cards have anything to do with the amazing success of both Topps and Stadium Club basketball in 1992-93? And lest Topps and Fleer think we are picking solely on them, how many packs of Upper Deck baseball do you think were sold in 1990 and '91 on the strength of autographed Nolan Ryan and Reggie Jackson cards?

Insert cards turn an innocent pack of cards into a lottery, and they are the most foolproof method yet devised of driving sales. Cardmakers love them and fall all over themselves trying to come up with more outlandishly conceived and designed insert cards. (Some personal favorites: Magic Johnson's favorite football players, from the '92 Impact football set; "Commanders of the Hill," from PX packs of Topps baseball cards; and the "Beam Team," in the '92-'93 Topps basketball sets, which ostensibly was based on a laser-light program that was touring NBA arenas but which never quite got that message across, stumping everyone who bought the set.)

The problem with insert cards is that they feed on themselves and the set that spawned them for their value. If all a set has to recommend it is its insert cards, its regular cards become meaningless, just a vehicle for carrying insert cards. And the regular cards in a set are its guts, the stuff that's meant to be collected and pored over and savored. If you don't collect a set for the set itself, by God, what's the sense of collecting?

Sorry about that outburst, but it's necessary for you to grasp the fallacy of insert cards. And if that doesn't do it for you, consider this: Very, very, very, very, very few insert cards start out cheap and get progressively more expensive; in fact, most times insert cards start expensive and get much, much cheaper as time goes on. You can buy Mickey Mantle autographed cards for a fraction of what they were going for originally; same with Pro Set Lombardi cards and Donruss Diamond Kings and practically any other major insert set you can name. As soon as that set has had its day in the spotlight, the bottom falls out of its insert cards and the people who buy and sell these things move onto the next one.

Ideally, the best time to sell an insert card is as soon as you get it. You may not get absolute top dollar for it, but you'll minimize your losses. Get it and bam! Turn it around. Or trade it out for whatever older material you can get your hands on. If you have a lot of insert cards, check the guides for the price trends for your specific cards. There are cases when the market in your insert cards absolutely bottoms out and you're going to be better off holding onto your cards. For instance, Lombardi Trophy cards are a little undervalued now—that's a point of reference, not a recommendation to buy every one you can get your hands on. But there aren't too many cases where you can be sure the market has absolutely hit bottom and there's nowhere to go but up.

After all, what does an insert card have going for it except scarcity? And in today's half-million-case world, is scarcity—even the purported ultimate scarcity of an insert card—really a concept worth discussing? The answers are nothing and no. Or as the Human Beinz would say, "No no no no no no no no no no no no no no no no no no no no no no (Nobody can do the BUGALOO like I do)."

Get rid of your insert cards. And while you're at it...

27

Sell every card you own that was made after 1989.

One of the more fashionable things armageddonist card writers like to do is pin down the date after which cards ceased to be valuable and began being a horrific waste of natural resources, a blot on the landscape, a zit on the nether cheek of the flower of womanhood...you get the picture. If you're a true hardcore armageddonist grouch and all-around iconoclast (and we won't name names except to say they didn't call it "The Old Grudge" for nothing), the date is somewhere between 8 B.C. and 1952. If you're less grouchy and prefer combing your hair down over your eyes and claiming you invented the trading-card hobby, the date is 1981. If you work for Fleer, the date depends on whether the story was written before or after you started working for Fleer. And if you're Kit Kiefer, it's like doing the big finale of the Hokey Pokey; either the whole body is in or the whole body is out. Baseball cards cannot have a line of demarcation drawn across them, with the stuff on this side of the line automatically more valuable than the stuff on that side of the line. You can make a very nice living buying and selling current-year cards, and you can get just blasted buying and selling '34 Goudeys. It's all in the approach and the tactics.

With that said, if you're going to pick a dividing line, 1989 is as convenient a place as any. In 1989 Upper Deck came along with a philosophy that was (caution: satire ahead) almost neo-Romantic in its scope, echoing the uncertain "do I wake or sleep?" mind-set of Keats, Shelley and the other major figures of the Romantic age and employing a distribution system that positively reeked of Kantian phenomenalism while still making sure that K-Mart got 10,000 cases. Upper Deck did change the rules of the game, and not at all for the better. After Upper Deck's successes, print runs rose, the number of collectors rose, the number of investors and shops and dealers and weekend card shows rose, and old women fell and couldn't get up. Everything got bigger and everyone bought the line and became convinced that things could only get better, and things got better for a time and then just deflated, leaving hundreds of thousands of cases of 1989-91 product absolutely stranded.

If you have quite a bit of this stuff—1990 Donruss, say, or even '91 Upper Deck—you're in a no-win situation. You're not going to get anything for it now, and you're not likely to do any better holding onto it for another 5 or 10 years. If you're a collector, and you put sets away from these years thinking they'd pay for a college education or a new home or what have you, don't be disillusioned with card collecting, but do toss out what you have and start over. You just bought the wrong stuff, that's all. No big deal; there's no way you could have known.

On the other hand, if your collection consists of top-grade Allen & Ginters and Old Judges and you're feeling quite smug about it, there's nothing that says you can't be a grotty old stick-in-the-mud, too.

28

Sell all your Upper Deck cards.

One of the authors (the one with the chin again) used to be the editor of *Baseball Cards* magazine, during which time he was not exactly the fair-haired boy in the eyes of the people who make trading cards. The people who make Donruss, for instance, would accuse him of trying to make nice-nice with Score, though the people who make Score were sure he was trying to score points with Topps, who didn't accuse him of trying to be nice to anyone but merely said, "Uh, can we get back to you on that?"

And everyone accused him of kissing up to Upper Deck except the folks at Upper Deck. They thought he was the Antichrist.

The fact that everyone thought he was picking on them ought to tell you two things: First, that editing *Baseball Cards* magazine is not a job for 14-year-olds with acne or anyone else with major self-esteem problems, and second, that anyone who could get every major card company to think that he was ripping on it so he could make points with its competitors has to be doing something right.

Which brings us to Upper Deck.

Upper Deck has found the recipe for making money in the card business. Leaving out the unimportant stuff, like the half-teaspoon of nutmeg, it goes something like: Make really good-looking cards, make lots of them, and then charge more for them than anyone has ever charged for cards in the history of cards. Bake for 40 minutes until a toothpick inserted into the center comes out clean. It's a good recipe—better than pumpkin-apple pie, even. Since its inception in 1989, Upper Deck has evolved into a card company worth a cool $1 billion.

That's not my number; that's the number placed on the company by a jury in Orange County, California, in a lawsuit brought by a lawyer who claimed he was entitled to 10 percent of the company in a handshake deal made with the original owners when the company was founded, and was awarded $33.1 million, so that number's inaccurate. Half of that $1 billion would be a little more like it.

But hey, billion or half-billion, the bottom line is that Upper Deck still makes and sells an awful lot of cards. And Upper Deck would rather you believe that it doesn't.

Upper Deck, as it begins to settle into middle age by card-company standards (which are an awful lot like dog years), is a frustrating company for card investors. Its cards are great for collectors to collect, but the numbers are all wrong for investors. Upper Deck makes too many cards and has since the outset. Complicating matters, many people have purchased Upper Deck cards thinking they were relatively scarce and would hold their values better than other card products, and those people look to be wrong. Not every Upper Deck card is in a tailspin, but enough are to give you reason to recommend a total sell-off of all your Upper Deck cards.

If you're looking for money, that is. If you're looking for beautiful cards, don't ever part with your Upper Decks. The upside to Upper Deck is that from the outset it has made a distinctive product that very often is the epitome of excellence in a baseball card. The photos jump out at you like no one else's (thanks to Upper Deck's advanced photo-doctoring technology), the set flows from photo to photo with grace, and even the chase cards mesh with the regular set. That could well mean that Upper Deck cards will remain the cards of choice over time, but you can't count on that. Beauty and base-ball-card values rarely go hand in hand.

Upper Deck is not the most wonderful card company that ever came down the pike. You wouldn't want Upper Deck to date your sister, for instance. As a maker of investments it stinks. But as a maker of baseball cards it's great. If you collect Upper Deck cards, more power to you; if you bought Upper Deck cards to turn them around, better start turning.

29

Sell all your Ken Griffey Jr. cards.

Kit Kiefer is the first person to admit that he likes Ken Griffey Jr. A lot. When it's his turn to draft a player in his fantasy-baseball draft, he takes Ken Griffey Jr. When pressed to name future first-ballot Hall of Famers, the first name off his lips is Ken Griffey Jr. He even has the plastic souvenir Ken Griffey Jr. sheet made by the auto-parts store that also made trading cards for a while, that's how much Kit Kiefer loves Ken Griffey Jr.

But even though Kit Kiefer loves Ken Griffey Jr., he says that now's the time to unload your Ken Griffey Jr. cards.

It must break his heart, and it does, but Kit Kiefer presses on with his recommendation nonetheless. Why? Because Griffey's time has come. As far as Griffey's cards are concerned, to quote the immortal Rodgers's and the immortal Hammerstein's immortal song from the immortal musical *Oklahoma*, "They've gone about as fur as they can go." They're wonderfully expensive, and if you have them and want to realize any sort of a profit from them, sell them right now. They have peaked, and though they may get more expensive they are not likely to get any more valuable.

Leave us explain. Some expensive cards lack value. They merely cost money and give you nothing in return. Other expensive cards cost money but offer in return the promise of appreciation. Those cards are valuable.

Valuable cards are valuable irrespective of age or grade. A '34 Diamond Stars Goose Goslin is valuable, not because it's a '34 Diamond Stars but because it's an undervalued card. The '34 Goudey Lou Gehrigs are not valuable, not because they're old but because their chances of significant appreciation are nil. And for a long time Ken Griffey Jr. cards were valuable because they promised more and better and looked to be able to deliver.

No longer. Ken Griffey Jr. is settling into the sort of career that will easily get him into the Hall of Fame, but the sort of career that will not continually shatter barriers and scale new heights. If he hits .312 with 30 homers and 115 RBI each year that's truly a wonderful thing, but after a time collectors will become accustomed to it and will not think it reason enough to buy his cards and drive them up in value every time he does it. As a result, Ken Griffey Jr. will likely have a career marked by superb consistency and flat card prices.

Our colleague Hal Hintze has done a marvelous study on this very subject. He finds that many players who have roller-coaster careers do better on the card scale than players who have straight-line careers. The reason: Once a card price goes up in value it tends to stay up, despite off seasons. But a good season after an off season tends to drive up the value of a card more than a good season after another good season would. So if Ken Griffey Jr. wanted to do good things for the prices of his cards, he would mix up his good seasons and his bad seasons. If he doesn't his cards will suffer.

There will always be a demand for Ken Griffey Jr.

cards because he is a good player and there are a lot of Ken Griffey Jr. collectors. But there isn't likely to be increasing demand and higher prices for Ken Griffey Jr. cards for another 10 years at the earliest, and by that time, who knows what shape the market will take? So sell your Ken Griffey Jr. cards now and feast on the profits. Your heart may say no, but logic will show you the wisdom of your ways.

30

Sell all your Nolan Ryan cards.

One of the great ways to start conversation, make new friends and test the resiliency of various barroom floors is to blurt out something like, "Y'know, Nolan Ryan really wasn't all that great a pitcher." Hoo DOGGIE! will the natives get restless over that one. And if you don't get tossed out of the place on your tush, you might actually get a real good argument going.

You can make a case—a real good case—that Nolan Ryan is more of a statistical freak than a great pitcher. He hasn't won a lot of games for the number of starts he's had, he's walked an incredible number of batters (he's the career leader in walks by a wider margin than he is the career leader in strikeouts), he hasn't pitched in a World Series since his early days with the Mets, he's only won 20 games once, and the only reason he holds as many records as he does is that he's been pitching forever. On the other hand, he does have 300 wins, he has thrown seven no-hitters, he has more K's than a whole skid of Alpha-Bits, and the very fact that he has been pitching forever is a marvel of one sort or another.

It's an interesting argument but it doesn't really settle anything. Nolan Ryan is going into the Hall of Fame whether fans want him to or not, and at this point they really, really do. Nolan Ryan has come to stand for something—fast pain relief without aspirin, primarily, but also things like endurance and perseverance and class—and his cards reflect his standing. They're real, real expensive, all except his stuff from the last couple of years, which is stuff from the last couple of years and consequently mostly trash. Fifteen hundred dollars for a rookie card? Five hundred bucks apiece for his '69 and '70 cards? No other cards from the very late '60s and '70s are as expensive as Nolan Ryan cards, and great as Ryan is, that's a structural imbalance in the card market that will eventually be corrected.

But not right away, and that's not a reason to sell your Nolan Ryan cards now, anyway. The reason to sell Ryan now is this: The market for Ryan cards is at or near its peak. His cards have made their big price run, and the forthcoming post-retirement price run and the pre-Cooperstown price run and the Cooperstown-year price run are going to be very small as percentages of the cards' current value. You're better off getting your money out of the cards now and turning your attention to other opportunities than holding onto your Ryan stash in hopes of 15 percent or 20 percent gains. With his cards as expensive as they are now, those sorts of gains just aren't there.

If you're a Ryan collector, fine. He's a very collectable ballplayer with a lot of interesting cards. But if you're a collector/investor heavily into Ryan multiples or very high-grade older Ryans, now might be the best time to move them out.

31

Sell all your Mark McGwire, Ruben Sierra, Ivan Rodriguez, Cecil Fielder, Joe Carter, Fred McGriff, and Dennis Eckersley cards.

You're getting a bargain here, an extra-value meal of a recommendation. Seven for the price of one, plus extra-large fries.

There's only one question you have to ask yourself when evaluating a player as a long-term card buy: "Is he going to make the Hall of Fame?" If the answer is no then you shouldn't buy that card; if the answer is yes you should.

The answer for all these players is no. Sometimes it's a very close no, but it's always a no.

McGwire is an excellent power hitter but not a great power hitter. His career numbers aren't apt to put him close enough to the greats to make him Hall of Fame material. While he's done some of the peripheral things that help put a borderline Hall of Fame candidate over the top—appeared in All-Star games, played in World Series, won a Rookie of the Year and an MVP award the same year—he's just not enough of an all-around player to land in Cooperstown.

Compare McGwire to Johnny Mize. Mize drove in runs by the carload, hit more than 400 home runs, hit for average and hardly ever struck out, and he had a heck of a time making it into the Hall of Fame. McGwire doesn't hit for average, strikes out too much and hasn't hit 400 home runs—yet. He may still, but don't count on it.

The competition for first basemen to get into the Hall of Fame is so fierce that not only McGwire but also Cecil Fielder and Fred McGriff may be excluded. Fielder is a power hitter in the old mold who may have simply started too late in amassing the sort of career numbers Cooperstown looks for from a first baseman. His story is interesting but the years he spent platooning with Fred McGriff may hurt him—just as they may hurt McGriff, who likewise has gotten a late start at greatness. All these first basemen need to be compared to Johnny Mize on the one hand (he got in) and Ted Kluszewski on the other (he didn't). Klu was a marvelous power hitter for a number of years, but he ran out of power and ran out of years too quickly. Any of these first basemen may need almost 500 homers to make it to Cooperstown, and they're not likely to get them.

Among the outfielders, Carter and Sierra are probably going to come up short of the Cooperstown standard, though Carter has all those runs batted in in his favor and Sierra is young enough to turn around a once-promising career. Rodriguez is included because he's a good catcher who has a lot more catching to do before he comes up smelling like Cooperstown, and his cards are priced so darn high right now it's too tempting not to tell you to sell them.

But among all the players, no call is harder than the call on Dennis Eckersley. Eck is an incredible pitcher. He won nearly 200 games as a starter and has saved more than 200 as a reliever. He won a Cy Young award. He won a couple Fireman of the Year awards. He pitched in three World Series and won a World Championship. He had a couple of seasons that statistically boggle the mind. But is that enough? Is that enough to make Dennis Eckersley a Hall of Famer?

His cards are certainly priced as though it is enough. But the fact is there may be a long wait for Dennis Eckersley to get into the Hall of Fame, if in fact he gets in at all. And if Eckersley starts languishing awaiting the call, his cards are going to plummet like rocks.

As we said starting this chapter, the only question you need ask when considering buying the cards of a veteran player with money-making in mind is, "Is this player going into the Hall of Fame?" When you have trouble making the call, as we have with Dennis Eckersley, it's a sign to let someone else take the risk and graciously bow out. There'll be other opportunities.

32

Sell Rookies of the Year the year after they become Rookies of the Year.

This may be a bit generic, but in general it's true: You should sell cards of any given year's Rookie of the Year as soon as possible after that person wins the award.

Walt Weiss? Should have sold him in 1989. Jerome Walton? Same story. Sandy Alomar Jr.? Him too. Chuck Knoblauch? A good player, but a slap-hitting infielder; anyone who thought there was a future in his cards beyond the short term was mistaken. Eric Karros and Pat Listach? They should have left your possession late in 1992, about the time they were driving the dregs of Stadium Club and Fleer Ultra. Even players like Jeff Bagwell and Dave Justice, who have found life beyond the Rookie of the Year award, were never better buys from a return-on-investment standpoint than they were in their rookie seasons. Everything after that has been sort of static.

The worst-case scenario is a

pitcher who wins Rookie of the Year. Moved any of those Butch Metzger rookies recently? How about Gregg Olson or Todd Worrell? Sure, Dwight Gooden has had a very good major-league career, but what if you had bought his rookie cards right after he won the Rookie of the Year award? What sort of investment would that have been?

One of the reasons to avoid Rookies of the Year, and to dispose of the ones you do have in your collection rather quickly, is that they unrealistically heighten expectations for themselves by winning the award. If Pat Listach had not won the Rookie of the Year award he would have been just another light-hitting infielder with speed but no power—and you know how far they make that ol' baseball-card Power-Meter rise. But in winning the award, Pat Listach suddenly became one of the game's elite, for a while at least, in the eyes of card buyers. Until that glow wears off, his cards will be too expensive to buy and will have absolutely no upside potential, and after the glow wears off, you wouldn't want to buy his cards anyway.

Sure, there are exceptions. Cal Ripken Jr. was an exception, but his rookie cards predate the sport-card tidal wave. Jeff Bagwell looks to be something of an exception. While his cards may not have a lot of upside potential, they certainly have a lot less downside risk than the cards of Dave Justice, for instance. Trade Justice out of Atlanta, send him to Kansas City or some such place, and see how he fares out of the vacuum-tube limelight.

Rookies of the Year make fine baseball players and surprisingly good house pets. The only way they make good baseball-card buys is if you buy into them early and sell them at the end of their rookie years. And the only way you can do that is to...

33

Subscribe to *Baseball America.*

Agood baseball-card investor needs surprisingly few resources outside of a good annual price guide, a good monthly price guide magazine, a good baseball-card-database program for his computer, an awful lot of money (and he doesn't necessarily need that, as we've shown), and more than 500 high-grade tobacco cards he found inside a bundle marked "T206 Reprint Set." One of those few resources is a wonderful periodical called *Baseball America.*

BA is a semi-weekly chronicle of the minor leagues that has reports from all the major-league teams' minor-league organizations, league-by-league reports and standings, free-agent-draft predictions and analyses, complete coverage of college baseball, and more minor-league statistics than you could shake a stick at, if that's your idea of a good time. It's utterly comprehensive and as much fun reading as a bunch of statistics and stuff from minor-league

baseball could possibly be. It can tip you off on minor-lea-
guers to watch for (great if you're buying minor-league
star cards or team sets) and can also give you a line on
the current rookies. It costs $38.95 a year and is worth
absolutely every penny. (And just to resolve those old con-
flict-of-interest bugaboos, yes, one of the authors occasionally writes for the publication. But he was an avid
reader of *BA* long before he was a writer.) If you can't
spring for $38.95, the *Baseball America Almanac,* pub-
lished annually, has all the pertinent information in one
neat package and is only $12.95.

So how do you use either of these publications?
First of all, you take a look at how the magazine rates
players, but don't put too much stock in their ratings.
Remember, you're basically looking only for power hitters
who can hit for average, too—Frank Thomas types. (We'll
save you a little trouble and name some names for you
later on.) Pitchers with great curveballs and infielders who
are already ready for the major leagues defensively are
nice, but they don't pay your bills.

Once you've perused their organization-by-organiza-
tion and league-by-league picks (which show up in the off-
season issues of the magazine, just in time for baseball-
card season), dive into the statistics yourself. It's like playing the stock market; you can see how someone else does
it or you can do it yourself, but if you do it yourself it's a
lot more satisfying. Hitters need to be judged on: 1) age
relative to the rest of the league; and 2) performance relative to the rest of the league. If a hitter in the Florida
State League has only 10 home runs halfway through the
season you might think he's not much of a power hitter.
Guess again: The FSL parks are huge, and a 20-homer
season is a monster in that league. Same with batting
average and home runs in the Eastern League. By the
same token, knock players' performances at Calgary,
Edmonton and Colorado Springs of the Pacific Coast
League, and El Paso of the Texas League, down a notch;
these are notorious hitters' parks and unreliable reflec-
tions of a player's true worth.

By the same token, if a player is tearing up the

Eastern League, hitting a lot of homers and posting a high average, and he's 26, what sort of prospect is he really? Renowned baseball number-crunchers like John Benson and Don Zminda figure that a player's peak performance potential usually comes when he's 26 and 27. A 26-year-old who's stuck in Double-A isn't going anywhere but maybe Triple-A—maybe. On the other hand, if a 19 year old is doing this stuff in Double-A, or if a Frank Thomas is doing it in Double-A just a year after being drafted, then you have to consider him a real comer.

As a for-instance, Juan Gonzalez did not have tremendous numbers throughout his minor-league career, but his minor-league career began at 16 and he was always one of the youngest players in whatever league he happened to be in at the time. You knew he was going to be good simply by seeing what he was able to do against more experienced competition. And darned if he wasn't good.

If you use *Baseball America* it will reward you with the next Juan Gonzalez or Frank Thomas. But you have to use it and work it. It won't tell you everything right up front.

34

And while you're at it, buy a subscription to *Sports Collectors Digest* or SCD Express.

We have a soft spot in our hearts for Krause Publications. It's the company that gave the authors their start (yes, it's the culprit), and it's the company that still puts out the best array of sports-collecting publications for the buck.

If you're serious about buying and selling, hopping on products and moving them, you need to have a subscription to *SCD*. It's the hobby's only weekly, and every issue is crammed—and we mean crammed—with ads from people looking to buy cards and sell cards and auction cards and trade cards. Sometimes it's a little daunting to go through, but it's a publication that has to be worked to be profitable. It's the place to buy your large lots of rookie cards. It's the place to go after buys in auctions. It's the place where your cards will likely appear if they're consigned to a mail-bid auctioneer. The articles tend to get pushed aside by the ads sometimes, but they're usually interesting and informative, and sometimes they're worth the price of the magazine all by themselves. There's also a price guide every issue, with the most up-to-date prices you'll find in print.

Notice we said "in print." If *SCD* is just not fast enough for you, consider SCD Express. It's a collector version of the SCD On-Line system which enables dealers to get the latest news, price-guide updates and business tips, and then buy and sell to their hearts' content with other dealers hooked up to the network. SCD Express gives you the option to make some of the same big deals they do, or put your own want ad on the system and scout around for cards you can't find any other way. It's relatively new and not entirely bug-free, but it's light years ahead of that other on-line system, which we'll call "Whizzo Butter," in terms of usefulness and user-friendliness.

Neither *SCD* nor SCD Express comes cheap. You'll have to shell out about $50 a year for an *SCD* subscription, and you could spend a good chunk of that each month following along with SCD Express. But all it takes is one good buy from either of these for you to recoup your investment—and from there on out it's pure profit.

35

Start buying stuff.

Stuff is cheap right now; the market for contemporary baseball cards is in a downturn and there are bargains to be had. While buying contemporary baseball cards means abandoning the idea that everything made after (pick one) 1952, 1981 or 1989 is trash and not worthy of your attention, trust us. It isn't all trash. Okay, okay, you're right; it is all trash. But so? Who said you can't make money off of trash? Topps does it. Donruss does it. Michael Bolton does it. So let's do it; let's fall in love.

Many, many chapters ago we remarked that you can get creamed buying '34 Goudeys or you can make money on current-year cards. A few chapters after that we talked about how to use *Baseball America* to plan your rookie-card buying strategy. You may not believe that you can make money on current cards and you may have forgotten that such things as rookie-card strategies ever existed, but you can and they do. The key to making money on current-year cards is to give the people what they want when they want it—which means you have to know what people want before they want it, always a fun task—and the key to having a rookie-card strategy is to wait for the rookie-card market to get itself straightened out. The card companies turned a nice little rookie-card market into mush by coming out with sets at all times of the year and all hours of the day and then filling those sets with every player who stood an outside chance of riding the bench at Triple-A that year, so that you had to buy rookie cards two or three years in advance of that player's making the big leagues, and then buy the right rookie cards to boot.

Major League Baseball, to its credit and our bewilderment (it had never shown signs of having a mind or a conscience or anything else but a couple of pockets and a Swiss bank account), finally stepped in and cleaned up the rookie-card market, telling the card companies it could only put players who had actually played major-league games in its set unless it paid extra for the privilege of slipping in a few can't-miss prospects. This will eventually right the baseball-card rookie market to an extent, but it's like reintroducing the timber wolf: It's going to take a while for the packs to mean anything again.

In the meantime, the general keys to making money on current-year cards are: pick wisely and buy early. Picking wisely is by far the harder of the two, because you're going to have to blaze a few trails and go against the flow. For instance, Fleer Ultra was such a hit in 1992 because the 1991 issue was so abysmally designed and promoted and sold and supported that most dealers took their solicitation for 1992 Ultra and chucked it. There wasn't much made, and consequently, all it took was a little blip of demand to get the market fired up. Same with 1992 Bowman baseball. Same with 1992 Stadium Club 3 football. Somewhat similar with Score Select baseball. These sets came into this world with a pariah label and got hot because of it. You as a card buyer have to be sensitive to that and react swiftly and accordingly.

That's why buying early is so important. You have to jump in ahead of everyone else. Once everyone jumps in, you have to jump out and jump into the next thing ahead of everyone else. That's where the money is made in modern baseball cards, but it's not an exercise for sheep. You have to be willing to stand by your convictions and be able to weather a few mistakes. You have to buy rookie cards as soon as they're available, and the cheaper the rookie the better. A 10¢ rookie card stands a much greater chance of going to 20¢ than a 50¢ rookie card stands of going to $1, and a $1 rookie card stands even less of a chance of making it to $2. Almost every year the player with the most expensive rookie card does not turn out to be the best player, so you have history on your side when you shun Gregg Jefferies in favor of Roberto Alomar, or choose Tim Salmon over Todd Van Poppel.

When you buy early it comes back around to buying smart. Choose players who look like home-run hitters and have a starting job waiting for them on a team that doesn't get much attention. Tim Salmon would be a perfect example, as would Jeff Bagwell. So would Jeff Conine and Jim Thome, but the jury is still out on those players. Avoid pitchers and heavily hyped players. You won't make money on Brien Taylor, Chipper Jones or Ryan Klesko; you just won't. Look for sleepers, and be willing to pay the price if your sleeper never wakes up.

It's an imperfect science, looking for shunned sets and overlooked players. You may lose as often as you win. But the wins will more than make up for the losses, and the whole enterprise will convince you that there is money to be made in current-year cards after all. And now, without further fanfare, a few picks from among the crop of current players.

36

Buy Carlton Fisk.

Pudge is technically not a current player currently (nice, huh?), but his career is so recently ended that he might as well be. Fisk ended things with more of a whimper than a bang, though he did break Bob Boone's record for most games caught in a career shortly before his release, shooting Boone's chances for making the Hall of Fame all to heck in the process.

But Pudge had a grand career, all things considered. He set the record for most home runs by a catcher. He never really hit for a great average, but he was a consistent .270 hitter good for 20-30 homers a year—for a lot of years. Fisk played 24 years, and played better to an extent as he got older. He played in a ton of All-Star Games, a couple of League Championship Series and a World Series, and is perhaps best remembered for giving his home-run ball the damn-you-stay-fair wave in the 1975 World Series.

That's the stuff that dreams are made of, the stuff of a Hall of Fame career, and no one's going to deny that to Carlton Fisk. The only questions concerning Fisk are when he's going to get into Cooperstown and with what sort of margin.

Some of our friends, people who dabble in trading cards and talk a lot of baseball very knowledgeably, claim that Fisk is the very sort of player who does not belong in the Hall of Fame. His career was based on longevity above all else, they claim, and maintain that any record he holds is the result of him staying around so darn long. To which we reply, "So?" Why did he stay around so darn long, smarty pants? Because he was bad? If Fisk had been a mediocre, dime-a-dozen catcher, he would have been out of baseball long before his forced exit in 1993. The very fact that he was still catching, and catching well, at the age of 45 is reason enough for him to be elected to the Hall of Fame. (Though Phil Niekro, we maintain, is a different story.)

Lest you think this is just idle haggling, the same arguments have coursed through the trading card biz, with the result being that Fisk cards have been taking a few shots to the dome lately. The 1972 Topps Fisk rookie had been selling for as much as $225-$250; now if you're lucky you can find one for half that. And with Fisk essentially out of the picture until his election, his card certainly isn't going to go up in value.

Two hundred twenty-five dollars might seem like a lot to pay for a card of a player who isn't in the Hall of Fame and isn't a lead-pipe cinch to make it there, but consider this: A Rickey Henderson rookie card is about the same price as a Fisk rookie and easier to find. Ozzie Smith and Andre Dawson rookie cards cost about $40 less, and neither of those players is as likely to get into the Hall of Fame as Fisk. A Dave Winfield rookie is $25 more, and Winfield is hardly superior to Fisk. George Brett and Robin Yount cards are more than twice the price of a Fisk rookie, and Yount is certainly an equivalent player to Fisk. Fisk's second-year card is a buy in its own right.

Carlton Fisk rookie cards could easily double in value in the next five years, and they're not as easy to find in top grade—on register, well-centered and sharp-cornered—as many comparable rookie cards. There are too many things in favor of Carlton Fisk's rookie cards for you not to buy.

37

Buy Paul Molitor.

Carlton Fisk is a sure thing for the Hall of Fame. Paul Molitor isn't. But there are plenty of compelling reasons for you to buy Paul Molitor's cards.

The first is that Molitor is still a very productive player. As a designated hitter and sometime first baseman for the most excellent Toronto Blue Jays, Molitor gets plenty of good pitches to hit and hits them. As long as he stays healthy—always a concern with Molitor—he's a cinch to hit .300 with double figures in homers and steals. He's been named the best baserunner in the American League several times in informal ballots of his peers, and he's one of the few players to be named to the American League All-Star Team at three different positions—first base, second base and third base. Molitor was a leadoff hitter throughout much of his career and amassed numbers in the leadoff spot second only to Rickey Henderson in quality and quantity. He'll likely finish his career with 2,700 hits and a batting average in the .300-plus range.

Is that the sort of thing that will get a player into Cooperstown? An old-time player, probably; a modern player, maybe. Modern players qualify for Cooperstown on sheer volume of stuff done: 3,000 hits over 25 seasons, 300 wins over 20, records for games pitched in or games played. Neglected is the quality of performances over a reasonably sustained period of time. The modern baseball noodler forgets that Rogers Hornsby and Ted Williams came up short of 3,000 hits for their careers, for instance, that Williams never cracked the 200-hit barrier one single season, or that Joe DiMaggio had only 2,200-plus hits and 361 homers for his career.

Speaking of Williams, he always used five years as his dividing line. Let a player do something special five seasons in a row, he used to say, and that's a special player. Paul Molitor has done it for more than five seasons in a row; he passes the Ted Williams test.

Quality per time at bat—that's another of Williams's favorite tests. What does a player do in relation to the number of times he gets to hit? DiMaggio may have had only 2,200 hits and 361 homers, but he hit .325 for his career, played in a tough park, and looked great doing it; you'd have to say he did about as much as any player could per time at bat. The same goes for Paul Molitor. No modern player gets more out of a time at bat than Paul Molitor. The only reason he has around 2,400 hits for his career and not 2,700 at the present time is that he missed the better part of three seasons to injury, just as Williams lost some of his best years to military service. Given that fact, the numbers he's put up and the numbers he's likely to finish up with, you'd have to say that Molitor is as certain a Hall of Famer as, say, Dave Winfield.

Considering all that, you'd expect a little more out of Molitor's rookie card, certainly. Molitor shares it with Alan Trammell (and we'll deal with him later), yet it's only a $70 item. Molitor's second-year card is all of 12 bucks. Heck, you'll pay that for a Stadium Club Travis Fryman card, and look what you get for your money: A genuinely kinda scarce card of a player who'll probably be in the Hall of Fame. Okay, it ain't a Zeenuts DiMaggio, but for 12 clams you can't expect it to be.

Steve Carlton has boiled down pitching to a glorified game of catch. If you get the ball past the hitter into the glove of the catcher you win the game. Buying the right rookie cards is like that, too. It all boils down to buying the rookie cards of players who will wind up in the Hall of Fame. And when you do that, and lay the game for keeps, the name of Paul Molitor keeps rising to the top.

38

Buy cards of Lou Whitaker and Alan Trammell.

Since 1978 Lou Whitaker and Alan Trammell have been the Tigers' double-play combination. No other combo in modern ball has been so durable or so productive. The two of them have combined for more than 500 homers and 2,000 runs batted in and have a batting average between them somewhere in the .280 range. That's heady territory for a shortstop/second-base combination; while it's not necessarily the stuff of Jackie Robinson and Pee Wee Reese, it's not the stuff of Mario Mendoza and Jack Perconte, either. And the show's not over yet: As this is being written, both Whitaker and Trammell have batting averages of better than .300 for the '93 season, with power figures that put them on a pace to hit 15-18 homers apiece. Seeing as both of them are two-thirds-time ballplayers, that's some nice work.

But nice work or not, it all comes back to the question, "Are these players going to make the Hall of Fame?" They certainly have a chance, though neither is a lead-pipe cinch. (Of course, if they were lead-pipe cinches they wouldn't be bargains, would they? You've got to take the bitter with the batter in this business, whatever that means.) Their numbers, certainly offensively and arguably defensively, are better than the top players who aren't in the Hall but maybe ought to be—Marty Marion, Bill Mazeroski and Nellie Fox. All those players were basically singles-hitting infielders; Whitaker and Trammell were the first of the new vanguard of power-hitting infielders. On the other hand, Whitaker and Trammell have not been clearly dominant at their positions throughout their career, and neither has set new standards for his position the way Ozzie Smith has. Smith may be a .260 hitter lifetime, but he has changed the way shortstops approach their work, and he has a ton of Gold Gloves and All-Star Game appearances. That's more than enough to get Smith into the Hall of Fame. Trammell and Whitaker have appeared in fewer All-Star Games, have fewer Gold Gloves, and have played most of their careers on the grass-and-dirt infield of Tiger Stadium, where redefining moments are hard to come by. They're not even the best offensive second baseman and shortstop of their league and era; you'd have to give the nod to Cal Ripken Jr. and Ryne Sandberg, though not by as much of a margin as you'd think. (Sandberg and Whitaker are particularly close.) But the evidence in their favor is: They've been very productive for a long time, they're in a position to be still more productive, they've been winners, and they meet the minimum requirements for their positions set by the likes of Pee Wee Reese, Luis Aparicio and Red Schoendienst.

Okay, so the verdict is in and it's a definite maybe on these guys. So what do you do with their cards? Buy them up, if you're smart. Trammell's on that delightful 1978 Topps rookie card with Paul Molitor (and lest we forget, Mickey Klutts and U.L. Washington) which goes for about $75. It's worth $75 if you believe either of them is a Hall of Famer; it's worth more if you think both of them are. Whitaker's on a Rookie Infielders card that same year with a less distinguished cast (Sam Perlozzo, Garth Lorg and Dave Oliver); that card goes for about $18 and could absolutely sneak up on people. As a flat-out bargain buy it's high on our list. For that matter, so are the '78 Burger King Tigers cards. These cards look like Topps cards but aren't (they're numbered differently, for one thing), and they are responsible for more letters to the editor than any topic this side of fluoridated water. Whitaker, Trammell and Jack Morris all have cards of their own in the Burger King Tigers set, which are as much true rookie cards as the cards in the big Topps set. Trammell's card is $20 and Whitaker's is $15, and they're both relatively scarce and worth buying.

Players like Trammell and Whitaker represent a gut check of sorts for card collectors. Are you willing to spend the money and take the risk on these players? If you are and are patient, chances are you will be rewarded. But if you hesitate, no one except us will think the worse of you for it.

39

Buy Willie Randolph cards.

Okay, here's a real gut check for you: How do you feel about Willie Randolph cards? Randolph fits in squarely with Mazeroski and Fox, though Randolph was arguably a slightly better offensive player and certainly played on more winning teams in his career. Randolph hit a solid .270-.280 every year, walked more times than he struck out, stole bases and did all the little stuff that makes baseball types squeal with delight. He was the consummate professional ballplayer on and off the field and the quintessential guy you want to have in your clubhouse.

So is that going to get Willie Randolph into the Hall of Fame? Not on the first go-round, certainly; the only guys who are getting in in their first round of eligibility are the established stars, the guys with 3,000 hits or 450 homers or 300 wins. After that, when the Veterans' Committee starts considering players from the current era, that's when all bets are off and a guy like Willie Randolph starts looking pretty good. He did all the things top-quality ballplayers do, and he did them for a long time. That will definitely get Randolph a lot of attention from his peers on the Veterans' Committee, and it might just get him a berth in the Hall of Fame.

If you're willing to wait 10 to 20 years for a player's cards to make a major move, Randolph just might be your guy. Randolph's rookie card is a $10 item in the 1976 Tops set, and after that his card prices fall off the face of the earth. Everything's a common, or just above a common.

We're not talking much money here. We're talking about buying cards that are commons now but could be much more than commons in a couple of decades. Even if they're not much more than commons in a couple of decades, they're worth having because they're late-'70s/early-'80s commons, cards that are due for a rise in price anyway.

When you look at it that way, Willie Randolph is a no-brainer. His cards are going to go up in value. The only question is whether you get the big rise or the little rise.

40

Buy Dwight Evans cards.

It's about time for a short chapter, so:

Everything that applies to Willie Randolph cards applies to Dwight Evans cards, though Evans is a much more likely candidate for enshrinement through the Veterans' Committee than Randolph. Evans, like Ozzie Smith, was a spectacular fielder who became an excellent hitter. He's in the top 50 all-time in runs batted in, and around the top 50 in most of the SABR-metric categories. His cards are more expensive than Randolph's; his rookie card, in the 1973 Topps set, goes for a hefty $60. Part of that price is due to the high-number series where the card resides; part of it is carryover from the Mike Schmidt rookie just a couple of doors down. But the price for the Dwight Evans rookie is soft; it will come down in the price guides, and it can be negotiated down right now. In the meantime, any other Dwight Evans cards aside from his rookie card are cheap, and worth buying simply for that fact.

Dwight Evans sure looks like an eventual Hall of Famer. If you're patient, he should reward you.

41

Buy the tough cards first.

It's an old rule from other fields, but it's a good one. Let's say you're putting together a collection of Mickey Mantle cards. There is a heck of a difference in price between his 1951 Bowman and 1952 Topps cards and his last cards. The difference isn't merely hundreds of dollars, but more like thousands or even tens of thousands.

The early Mantles are easily the keys to the collection and it does you little good to say, "Well, maybe I can afford them in a couple of years," as the odds are that the early Mantles—or any other key cards for that matter—will have risen in price at least as drastically as your ability to pay. Moreover, when you go to sell a collection, the cards that the dealer will examine first and more carefully are those key cards, the ones that are tougher to find and afford. It does your collection and finances no good whatsoever to cut corners on the expensive cards.

Sure, it's a tough rule to live with as your temptation is to want to get a lot of cards and get them fast, but the really astute investor/collectors resist that temptation and in the long run generally assemble their collections for far less money. Consider a 10 percent rise in the price of Near Mint Mantles. The combined Near Mint price of 1951 Bowman and 1952 Topps Mantles is around $47,000. The 1968 and 1969 Mantles combine for a price of about $400. A 10 percent increase in Mantle prices costs you $4,700 if you don't have the 1951 and 1952 and about $40 if you are missing the 1968 and 1969.

Even if money isn't the issue, buying the keys first makes sense if you want to finish a collection in a reasonable period of time. Take a baseball type collection in which you try to get one of each type of baseball card ever produced. You could start by acquiring dozens of types going back to 1887, but if you spent all of your immediately available funds in the process and then could not afford a true rarity like a T214 should one become available, you might end up putting the completion of your collection back years waiting for the next one. Some hockey cards are extremely difficult as well and not to have the funds ready when you need them for your collection means a lengthy delay in completing your set.

Yes, it's frustrating and initially slower, but on all counts, buying the tough cards in a collection first makes a great deal of sense.

42

Sell freebies.

Go to a big convention with card producers and guess what? You'll almost certainly be rewarded for your efforts with a gift of sorts in the form of some type of special cards produced as giveaways for that show.

Hot little goodies in hand (sometimes after spending what seems like an eternity in line waiting to get them), the immediate question is: What do you do with them? It's hard to believe anyone seriously has a question about that. Dealers and sometimes other collectors will offer to buy these cards, since they usually feature hot rookies, major stars or Hall of Famers. On rare occasions the prices offered get up close to triple figures, yet people resist selling.

For some strange reason people seem to think that the sports-card market is better than real life, a glorious place where every hit is a home run and every field goal is good unless the other team is attempting the kick. It's not. In fact, it's not even as good as the real world, where in theory you get what you pay for. In sports cards, more often than not you get less.

Think about it: Rightly or wrongly, the way most people determine card values is through price guides. Do the price guides list every incidental issue handed out at a show, inserted in a case of Diet Pepsi or included with an economy size bag of rat poison? Of course not, and they are not likely to start because card companies can produce special cards faster than computers and humans can catalog and price them. So they're not in the catalogs, and to many people that means they don't count.

Are the poor misguided folks who buy only those cards listed in the catalogs likely to change their ways? Probably not, and in the case of most promo cards they're probably better off, as generally after a day or two of excitement the demand vanishes leaving little chance to sell them for the big bucks offered for a few hours when they first appeared.

The message is a very simple one. If someone gives you cards at a show, unless they fit in your collection, take any offers you can get for them. Your chances of selling them later for even more money are somewhere between slim and none.

43

Sell all post-1975 cards.

It's the supply, stupid! Just carve that notion into your brain and repeat it as if you were running the Clinton campaign. Why? Because that's all you need to know—but for the sake of increasing the length of this book, and because it's a couple hours until dinner, I'll explain some more.

Yes, this is getting boring, but supply and demand determine price. Great art, quality rookies, geographical demand and probably even large family size can all affect demand for specific cards, but if the demand is still exceeded by the supply the price is headed straight down, even if everyone in the Norm Siebern Chowder and Marching Society buys his cards until they have to move out of the trailer and into spacious new quarters at some apartment complex just to accommodate the overflow.

Now, the problem with all of the favorite cards of most of today's collectors is that they were made after 1975.

It's not exactly an age problem, it's a supply problem. The market supply of these cards is not yet complete or anything like it. You see, out there in sheds and garages and mysterious hiding places like kids' closets lie hidden hoards of cards dating from 1975. If you think that's bad it get worse.

The situation is compounded by the fact that in those hoards are cases and cases of unopened boxes. Yes, Virginia, CASES! Ozzie Smith rookies in Mint, Michael Jordan rookies, Wayne Gretzky rookies and all the others from all the sports. They are still out there waiting to be discovered. Okay, so it's not the Holy Grail or anything like that, but it's semi-precious and a potential problem when it comes to dramatic price increases for cards since 1975.

Now it's not as though all this unopened material is by definition going to destroy the market for Michael Jordan rookies—far from it, because demand for hot superstars can still easily outpace any new supply. But they are the exception.

In reality, things get especially dangerous from about 1984 on, as by that time people were setting aside cases in large number and the pace increased with each year that followed.

It should be pointed out that the situation is most critical for baseball, as putting away cases of hockey, football and basketball came into vogue a few years later. Even so, it's safe to assume that if the cards were made after 1985 there are still plenty of them residing in unopened cases all over the country. It may not happen today or tomorrow, but sooner or later a lot of those cases are going to be opened. That will increase the supply of many of today's hottest cards, and that can't be good for prices.

44

Buy your own deals.

Wealth, travel to exotic locations, doing something you love—yes, you too can become a card dealer. The problem with the picture is that the image has little to do with the reality of countless days in airports waiting for planes that are hours late and hotel food which tastes the same from New York to San Francisco.

There is also a little matter called money. To have a decent-sized card business today costs money—a lot of it, what with cases as far as the eye can see, $40,000 Mantle cards and card shows every weekend serviced by airlines and hotels who sometimes seem to think the word recession means, "Stick it to these people, they're on business anyway."

So maybe being a card dealer isn't really for you after all—at least not on the national level. The fact is it may not be for too many on a local level, either. But even on a limited budget and with limited time, there are still ways to do things dealers do and make money at them as well.

You don't have to have a major card store to spend a few dollars and take out advertisements in local papers, weekly shoppers and other creative means of reaching people. Heck, it's even a time-honored tradition; the first card dealers in the country got their starts doing it that way. Some virtually went door-to-door asking if people had old baseball cards, and that was at a time when card dealers substituted one step below the local garbage man.

Even in today's marketplace, where every town with a zip code seems to have two card shops, there is still room to make some money buying other people's cards.

The number of card shops scattered around the country can be very misleading. Take even a small collection to most and they really aren't interested in buying it. Operating on extremely limited budgets, they have most of their funds tied up in the sets and cases of the past few years so unless a deal is close to extraordinary they just aren't interested. That may be where you fit in.

The problem is that working out of your home, you have to understand that after you buy someone's collection you still have to sell it somewhere and that somewhere is to a dealer. To do that you have to know what dealers are paying for almost any type of card, you have to know *quickly*, and there is no rule of thumb that always applies.

A nationally-known dealer I called one time about a football card lot said, "They're slow, don't pay more than 25 percent of book price," but that was football and just one type of that and only one grade of *that*, so it was hardly a universal pricing guideline.

That said, if a national dealer isn't too keen about buying certain cards at 25 percent of their book price it's safe to assume you have to pay a lot less. After all, you'll have expenses in selling collections even if you just ship them to dealers and wait for their checks.

To many, the notion of someone selling a collection for say 10 to 15 percent of its theoretical book value may seem absurd, but it happens all the time and someone with a bit of extra cash could easily be one of the buyers.

If you do buy such collections and you've paid the right price for them, you can usually make some money in the deal, keep a couple cards for your own collection and still manage not to have your money tied up too long. Plus, going through someone else's collection can be fun and, in the case of original childhood collections, educational as well since you'll be able to see what cards popped up in what numbers for this one person as he or she opened packs in years gone by.

45

Sell rookies when they're hot.

Eric Davis was the rage. He could do everything, and his rookie card absolutely took off. First $10, then $15 and then $20, and nobody could get enough Eric Davis rookie cards. Smart owners could have bought new cars with the killings.

Then the problems appeared. Eric Davis could do everything, with the possible exceptions of staying healthy and staying motivated. Demand for his rookie card vanished almost as fast as it appeared. It's probably possible to sell an Eric Davis rookie today, but it's unlikely you'll get anything close to $20, unless it's in Fijian dollars.

The moral of the story is simple. When you're dealing with modern rookies from any sport you sell when the selling is good. If you get greedy, more often than not you lose. Even if you sell before the top, would you be better off taking $13 for a Davis rookie or waiting too long and trying to sell it

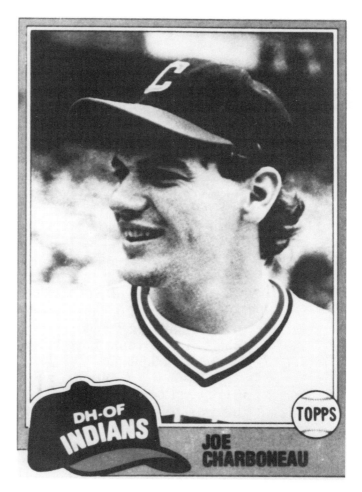

today?

The lesson is especially true if you have a lot of rookies of a given player. If you really think that Shaq is the next coming of Wilt Chamberlin, swell. Why not sell some of your rookies so that you get your money back? You can spend those dollars on something else and hold on to the rest which are now free. Then if Shaq is better than Wilt you still have plenty of profit, but if he's a bust you've lost nothing.

46

Sell cards with silly premiums.

Try a few of these on for size. A Jim Grabowski rookie lists at over $3. A Cazzie Russell brings over $7. The Stanley Cup brings about the same and Marvelous Marv Throneberry brings over $10.

These aren't even the worst examples, but they are typical of some prices that just don't honestly make a whole lot of sense. Yes, Marv Throneberry produced what could only be described as an exciting season for the original Mets. Some of the thrills centered around his base running, like the time he missed first on one of his very, very rare triples. Some of the thrills came from his fielding, which was really quite remarkable for its creativity if nothing else. But $10!!! There were small children chortling with glee watching the exploits of Throneberry and his co-conspirators on the original Mets that year. Sure, you pay good money for *Naked Gun* movies, but you don't expect someone to pay you money later for the ticket stub.

As for the others, Cazzie Russell was a great college player and not a bad pro, maybe even a good one. Jim Grabowski was an effective college back who had far fewer moments as a pro. The Stanley Cup, while perhaps the most recognized trophy in team sports, just doesn't seem like the sort of thing a card collection should be built around. Yet all these cards bring pretty healthy price premiums over the prices for commons in the same sets.

Consider some other facts. There are premiums for virtually every rookie card no matter how bad the player. Admittedly they drop over time, but we're still talking about $65 for the rookie card of another Mets immortal, Jim Hickman. Yankees do about as well and there are some cards that get good price premiums for no apparent reason whatsoever.

It's a free country and you're entitled to pay such premiums if that's what you'd like to do. Just don't expect to make any money doing it.

There are probably plenty of reasons for wanting a Stanley Cup or Marv Throneberry card; some of them may even be valid. The fact remains, however, that if you are concerned about making money you pay extra money for Hall of Famers, great condition and great rarity and little else—even if you loved Marv Throneberry and all he did wrong on the original Mets.

47

Sell #1 draft picks.

There's nothing quite like draft day in sports. ESPN addicts sit spellbound as their favorite team adds the missing piece to their championship puzzle. At least that's how it seems when you listen to the local analysis from each city around the league.

Of course there's a problem. Lots of mistakes are made and a lot of disappointments occur as high-priced rookies become overpriced veterans.

Collectors play the same game but for more modest stakes. One rookie card of a given player is harmless fun, but 100 of that player is a significant investment and 1,000 of them can be something closer to a financial time bomb just waiting to go off in your wallet.

Let's do some realistic evaluating of the situation. All professional sports teams pay scouts and other pros a lot of money to try to pick the winners from each year's crop of rookies. They still manage to make plenty of mistakes, yet in picking rookies for investment you attempt to do the same thing. Can you possibly expect to do better than the scouts, player personnel directors and coaches of this world?

Of all the sports, basketball tends to be the one where first round draft picks are most likely to succeed. Even so, teams draft other players before they draft Michael Jordan. In other sports the situation is even less accurate: For example, only about 50 percent of the players selected as the number one pick in the NFL draft actually go on to become starters and fewer still become stars. The odds of selecting stars goes down even further in hockey and baseball.

Professional teams can settle for solid ballplayers and still consider a draft successful. But a card buyer has to get stars and Hall of Famers to make a profit. There simply are not very many of either in the average draft and in some cases there are none. Even the best drafts will produce only a small number and those drafts are basically limited to basketball and football. The odds are stacked heavily against much investing success through first round draft picks.

The second consideration is that the prices of first round draft picks' rookie cards tend to be significant. The real money made off rookie cards is made by the 10¢ surprises who turn out to be stars and not the $5 top selections. Buy enough expensive top picks and you're far more likely to end up with some big dollar losses that will cancel out the few picks who lived up to their promise.

Under the circumstances, the main way to make money off top draft picks is by selling them quickly before they have to justify their lofty status on the field, the court or the ice.

48

Buy auction lots.

We can hear you already. A Gehrig jersey for, say, $250,000 or a T206 Wagner for a modest $400,000. How does the average person ever hope to buy at auctions, much less get good deals in the process?

Well, if it were easy everyone would do it, so you can expect to do a lot of work, but the truth is you can buy at auctions of any size and still make money in the process. But you have to know what you are doing and you have to be willing to spend the time required both to study auction catalogs and to do the actual bidding.

The small mail-order or phone auctions found in the pages of *Sports Collectors Digest* each week are pretty simple. There you simply follow the rules and make certain the lots you win are really as presented. As they are not major national events, bidding is not as intense, and the lots are more likely to be the sort of items most collectors and dealers are used to handling or grading.

It might come as something of a surprise, but some of the best deals for a small collector or dealer have been known to come out of some of the largest and most important auctions. Yes, the very ones with the Wagner, the Gehrig jersey, the Ruth bat and all the other stuff that seems to belong in a museum.

But how do you, the little guy, compete with people who can spend $200,000 or $400,000 on the lots they want? You don't, but remember they don't want every item in the auction and that leaves room for you and everyone else. Okay, so the lots you can buy are not exactly the ones featured on the cover of the slick auction catalog or in the color pictures inside, but they're there all the same, and sometimes they are far better deals.

Here's what to look for in those fancy catalogs. More often than not, buried away amidst all the five- and six-figure treasures are lots that the company had to take from major consignors simply to get those items in the color pictures.

Typical examples of such lots are lesser known player jerseys and cards—sometimes many of them in large lots that the auction company doesn't really care about and that are thrown in with low or no minimum bids. Such lots are frequently overlooked by the people at the auction as they are not pictures in the catalog, and frankly the sort of people who are willing to fly across the country to bid on a Babe Ruth jersey are not likely to care about 100 T206s in VG. Maybe they don't care, but with a little bit of luck you can buy a lot like that or the VG 1953 Mantle for very little money simply because no one else bothered.

To be honest, it doesn't happen often, but when you do "steal" such lots you can almost always make very good money and do so very fast—an ideal combination.

49

Be wary of memorabilia.

The biggest-ticket items in any major auction are generally not cards. They are jerseys, bats, autographs and a host of other items clumped under the heading of memorabilia.

If they are all as advertised, some of these things should be in Cooperstown and not in the living rooms of America. The operative word in the previous sentence is "if"; questions abound as to just what items are real and what aren't. In fact, there have even been national reports of items priced at six-figure dollar amounts being withdrawn from an auction due to questions of authenticity.

In today's market, with the high prices being paid, it's a serious matter to know just how well authenticated a jersey, bat or autograph is for later sale. Just because an auction catalog offers the item does not by definition mean its authenticity is beyond question. The same applies strongly to private sales.

Perhaps the most precarious area of the market is autographs. It has long been suggested privately by dealers that a day would come when the autograph field would erupt in scandal. After all, if a player can make a good living signing his name, should it come as any surprise that an unscrupulous individual would make an even better living signing the name of a player or players? Moreover, protection against such fraud is limited at best.

Experts, such as they are, tend to be self-appointed based on their years of experience. But they are hardly disinterested and are subject to grave limitations in their expertise.

Some day sign 10 checks without concern as to whether your signatures will match, then check the results. Do any two of the signatures look precisely alike? In some cases, on irregular surfaces you may even do it so badly that your name appears to be spelled incorrectly. Consider athletes in a hurry signing everything from jerseys to balls to equipment to cards to heaven knows what using everything from good surfaces to people's backs for support. Are you going to get anything even close to matching signatures? Of course not, yet that is our standard today for determining both good and bad signatures. It's probably wrong in both cases.

Our information on jerseys, game-used bats and the like is a little better, perhaps, but not much. There are company records, which, combined with known examples of things like Ruth bats and Cobb jerseys, are a starting point. Of course, jerseys change, as do players' preferences in bats and gloves, so the system in all cases is not without its problems. The experts in the field are generally well-intentioned but strangely enough seem to have a difficult time recognizing what a consumer advocate would consider a conflict of interest.

All of this is not to suggest that these fields are rife with fraud and abuse, although some might well go that far. Rather what is being pointed out is the potential for problems, which could spell trouble both for resale and profits.

By comparison, cards have few such difficulties.

Yes, there have been counterfeits, but they are usually spotted very quickly. Moreover, solid information is available. Trimming and restoration are the prime concerns, yet at least in the case of the former there are plenty of "good" examples around for comparison.

It's quite possible that you can make money with memorabilia, but the dollars tend to be high and the risks for losses out of proportion to those you'd incur with a similar amount spent on cards. Under the circumstances, unless the authentication is without any potential hitch, the prudent course is to take your profits or cut your risks and get into cards or something else.

50

Avoid duplication.

Is there any reason for having more than one of a specific card? So far, at least, no one has presented a compelling case outside of immediate family members for having 50 Denny Neagle cards. Even dealers don't generally have multiples of most cards, with the exception of modern cards for team sets or heavy demand from regulars for a fan favorite.

It's one thing to collect all the cards of Wilt Chamberlain, but it's quite another to collect extras of some of the cards that would be included in such a collection but people do it perhaps figuring that Chamberlain, Mantle, Howe, Unitas or whoever will be in such terrific demand that they can profit later. It doesn't often happen that way, or if it does, your money could usually have been better spent elsewhere.

The situation is even more pronounced with modern cards. Wave after wave of youngsters and even adults haunt the aisles at card shows looking for book value on 17 Jose Canseco rookies. There are rarely if ever any takers, as dealers have learned that there is little financial gain in taking too large a position in one player.

While speculators seem to think multiples of a given player represent greater opportunity, most dealers view rookies a little like a financial game of pass the bomb. With each modern rookie representing a bomb ready to go off, why have too many of them?

No matter what the set, there are very few cards that are likely to justify someone's investment in duplicates. Even if a few actually do go up significantly in price they are usually balanced by others that sink to their raw cardboard value. Moreover, looking at copy after copy of the same card is not exactly inspiring.

Look at it this way: Most hobbies cost money. If a sports-card collection breaks even and provides you with hours of fun you're way ahead of the game. So why not have some fun and leave speculation in large quantities of one thing to people who deal in futures contracts of onions or silver.

51

Buy Curtis Joseph.

Sad but true. Goalies do not bring big bucks. Oh sure, there are a couple exceptions, but the sad fact is that people don't like goalies much more than they like solid defensemen. There may be a small band of goalie supporters out there who had relatives frightened by hockey pucks or whatever, but the vast majority of people simply view goalies as bodies on which to place decorative masks.

If, however, you happen to be one of that rare breed, or if you happen to be looking for a different adventure with your money, a goalie might well be the item for you.

In the current world of netminders, one young goalie worth watching is Curtis Joseph of the Blues. Joseph has had a few solid seasons, but he really began to draw attention in 1992-93 Stanley Cup playoffs when he far outshone everyone on the Blues. Had it not been for Joseph, the Blues would have been gone quickly and convincingly. As we were shown in their game-seven loss, Joseph accomplished it all without a lot of help. He clearly has that air of big-game goalie about him.

Admittedly, neither Joseph nor any other goalie (all of whom look a little like brightly decorated rat boys waiting to stop screaming pucks with their sticks, pads or body parts) is a great investment, but if you're going to have a goalie in your portfolio he might as well be a good one.

52

Cut losses.

Okay, so you took a beating on Dwight Gooden or held Bo until after the injury. Those things happen to everyone. Somewhere out in the cosmos there are 5,000 Joey Meyer cards still looking for a home as Joey was going to be the next Babe Ruth. Well, in a way he was, but waist size doesn't compensate for the lack of a .320 average or say 57 home runs.

Things have a way of going wrong. This is why teams drafted Brian Bosworth or other players when Michael Jordan was still unclaimed. Heck, someone traded the rights to Joe Barry Carroll for Robert Parish and the rights to Kevin McHale. If you did that with their cards of just that year you traded traded $21 for a buck so it happens to the best of us.

A pro team has to live with the consequences of such a faux pas. At press conference after press conference the general manager gets asked about such moves. He generally shuffles his feet and looks down like he's trying to find a missing navel. After all, he's hurt his team and probably blown a few million dollars in the process. It's not a pretty sight.

You, on the other hand, don't have to explain your mess, but more importantly, you don't have to live with it. So you take a big position in Drew Bledsoe cards, or maybe Paul Kariya is your pick. On paper they look great, but maybe, just maybe, things don't work out. The fact is, you've lost the money you spent. Forget the fact that the catalog says your $2 per card is now 75¢ per card. We know better; it's about 1¢ per card at best. Realistically, they are probably unsaleable. You know how to make the bad situation worse? Easy, hold onto those losers. Heck, if they haven't made it after five seasons, is there really any reason to expect a change? Of course not, but people hold on anyway.

There's a great thing on the back of most cards. It's called a birthdate where it tells you when the player depicted on the front was born. It's not unlike the signs in bars that say if you were born after whatever date in 1973 you cannot drink. In the case of athletes you just change the wording. Subtract 25 years from the current year, and if the athlete was born before that date and is not clearly on a Hall of Fame path, SELL! Don't wait for the next eclipse, don't wait for the next left-handed president, don't wait for anything, just sell the blooming cards and be done with it. Get what you can, and if you can't get anything just give them away. It takes good money to store them and why waste it on a losing proposition?

Sure, it's not easy to admit you were wrong, but in the long run it's far better to swallow and learn from your mistakes than to compound them.

53

Sell Reggie White.

Does this guy look like the greatest defensive end in the history of the NFL? Even if he does, can he possibly live up to expectations? The answer to that question is almost certainly a resounding no.

Let's face it: The expectations for Reggie White in Green Bay are far from modest. Packer officials immediately began talking playoffs while fans started to book hotel rooms for the Super Bowl. Had all this nonsense been isolated to the greater metropolitan Green Bay area (a few restaurants, some bars and a gas station), no one would have cared, but the Reggie White story was bigger than that.

Reggie White wasn't like any normal free agent. No, White went on a national tour worthy of Michael Jackson. A lunch with team officials here, a chat with the governor there and hoards of media everywhere. Small wonder the Pope scheduled Denver after the signing of the Reggie

White. Who would want to compete with the White Tour '93 for headlines?

Anyway, after the glorious media event everyone with a television had to know that the previously not-that-well-known White was the greatest single football player since man first kicked pig. His card prices were certain to react accordingly even if the Pro Football Hall of Fame still grimly stood by their selection procedures.

Now let's be realistic about the Reggie White thing. First, he would not make a good governor of Georgia. Second, he will help the Packers. Third, that help will not produce a Super Bowl; it's worth noting White did play for a pretty decent Philadelphia club that didn't make the Super Bowl prior to the Packers taking out a mortgage on the Fox River Valley to sign White. Lastly, good though he may be, even great though he may be, Reggie White is no Dick Butkus or Joe Greene. Deacon Jones maybe, but Butkus no way!

If you have Reggie White cards and can sell into a

frenzy, do it. You can always buy them back later when Reggie White is a routine Hall of Famer and not the Reggie White Tour of '93.

54

Buy Brian Leetch.

Do we like Brian Leetch? Does a kid like Christmas? Moreover, we like him a whole lot more now that he and the Rangers have had that nightmare they tried to pass off as a season in 1992.

But let's go back to 1990. That was the year the Rangers topped the NHL in points. They took two games from Pittsburgh in the Stanley Cup playoffs before falling to the Penguins, and Leetch was the top defenseman in the league. Then along came 1991.

Leetch got hurt and with his injuries went the Ranger fortunes. He came back around mid-season, but he stepped out of a cab, and that was it for the year and the Rangers (maybe now they will repair the streets in New York). It was a disaster of epic, no, of biblical proportions, and heads rolled. Probably the most talented team in the NHL wound up bringing up the rear of the division.

Leetch healed in 1992, and the

Rangers—well, the Rangers have talent, they have money to buy more talent and they have a mission since none of their players was alive when the last Stanley Cup was held by a Ranger. Heck, their parents probably weren't alive when the last Stanley Cup was carried aloft by a Ranger, but that's another story.

Anyway, as Leetch goes, so go the Rangers. He anchors the defense and he puts the power in their power play. If there is to be a Stanley Cup in the hands of a Ranger in this lifetime or even in the lifetime of the planet it will almost certainly be the work of Brian Leetch.

Yes, the Rangers winning is something of a long shot, but with Leetch it could happen and if it does his cards will absolutely take off. Moreover, he's in the perfect position right now for buyers, since he's young. One lost season won't kill his Hall of Fame chances, and with that lost season his prices are down or at least soft. You can't ask for a better situation. Just remember, we're talking about a potential New York championship here and one that ends a 50-plus year drought. That's big anywhere, but in New York—wow!

55

Buy Alonzo Mourning.

While buyers hovered around the Shaq like ants hovering around a piece of cake with purple frosting at a national insect convention, a potentially great center was being ignored or something close to it.

In any other year Alonzo Mourning would have been rookie of the year. But in 1992, Mourning held his own against Parish and Ewing in the playoffs with a determination that can only spell good things in the years ahead.

In the process, he and not O'Neal gained playoff experience, which in the NBA is on a whole different level than during the regular season. Sure, the Hornets were eliminated by the Knicks, but they themselves eliminated Boston and Mourning impressed everyone while learning from crafty veterans in the process. As the years go on he should be that much better, as should Larry Johnson, who is the perfect complement in a potentially dominant Charlotte front line.

Like any rookie, it's too early to tell about Mourning, but he seems to have all the tools and an attitude that makes him play hard all the time. Add that to a team that has already showed real promise and you have all the ingredients for a player with a big future on a winning club. How the Hall of Fame loves that combination.

56

Sell the Shaq.

L et's get real. Shaquille O'Neal had an excellent rookie season. He even deserved rookie of the year honors (can you name the last five winners of that honor)? He may even become a legitimate Hall of Famer, but there's a rub.

Actually there are a few rubs. The opening rub is that right now Shaq is at the height of his popularity. In a rookie-crazy world he has a problem, which is that he's no longer a rookie. Lest you think that's not an issue, do the names Larry Johnson or Dikembe Mutombo mean anything to you? If they don't, why are you messing around with basketball cards in the first place?

Secondly, the beloved Shaq is already at very high prices, prices like those brought by David Robinson (who happens to be a pretty decent center himself), prices similar to those brought by the likes of Patrick Ewing and Hakeem Olajuwon, who just happen to be better centers than O'Neal and who were all pros before O'Neal was even an oversized recruit at LSU and who are now in the top few for MVP while O'Neal is grabbing rookie-of-the-year awards.

Thirdly, there is not a spot in the Hall of Fame for someone just because he is capable of pulling down baskets, backboards and whatever else is standing. Heck, if a rhinoceros could jump it could do that too. No, to get to Springfield, O'Neal is going to do what he did this year, only better and for a very long time, and then it would also help if he won a title or two of some type. That's a lot of "ifs" and while O'Neal is young enough to get them done, he's also currently riding a publicity wave that is the envy of every professional athlete other than Michael Jordan.

Sorry, Shaq followers, but all signs are that he's peaked in price and popularity for a while. Save a couple of his rookies if you must, but sell the rest, take the profits and consider yourself lucky.

57

Buy Teemu Selanne.

What? No, Teemu Selanne is not a new cold cut. He is, however, the guy who outscored Eric Lindros in his first year. In fact, it wasn't just Lindros. Teemu Selanne pretty much outscored everyone. He came close to outscoring a few teams and he did it all in the privacy of Winnipeg.

With the appropriate apologies to our friends in Winnipeg, it is not the media mecca of the Western world. Heck, it's not even the media mecca of Canada, and that means Teemu accomplished his great feats with relatively little attention save for ESPN, which seemed to take special delight in his achievements.

Clearly, Teemu Selanne is a bit of a gamble as a young player on a lesser-known team. Even if NHL defensemen can't shut him down (and who has ever stopped a Selanne before) there's a serious question about whether or not anyone outside of Winnipeg will ever hear of his exploits.

Fear not, Selanne followers; it's ESPN and a new aggressive NHL leadership to the rescue. No, Selanne will not get the same exposure as he would in New York or Los Angeles, but he won't be ignored, either. If he keeps scoring goals (and Lord knows he's done that everywhere), Teemu will be a household word and his prices will do just fine.

58

Buy Jeff George.

The good news is Jeff George isn't going to cost you an arm or leg. Fact of the matter is, he isn't going to cost you any body parts and probably not even a large fry at your favorite fast food establishment.

There is also a little more good news about George. He's the physical talent the Colts thought he was when they traded about 1,500 pounds of body parts in the form of some really good players to get George.

And one final bit of good news about George is that he's finally got an offensive line that resembles an offensive line more than it resembles the Maginot Line, so he could actually stay healthy enough and have long enough to find some pretty decent receivers. Plus there's a defense in Indianapolis that can actually get him the ball often enough to put up the sort of numbers that could see him make his mark in the NFL.

But like everything else in life,

there's some bad news. The worst of it is George doesn't seem to understand the good news about George. Just at the time when his career should really skyrocket, George wants to go someplace else. Maybe George likes defensive linemen trying to rip off his body parts.

It's strange—every time you think of George you almost have to think of those awful words in Indianapolis, "John Elway." For those who have short memories, Elway was going to be a Colt too. Except he whined, moaned and otherwise threw a tantrum worthy of any kid who just got two checklists in a $2.49 pack of cards.

Elway went to Denver, where he found Hall of Fame numbers, no Super Bowl ring and a vicious local media— funny how guys like George, Elway and Eric Dickerson find vicious local media everywhere, isn't it?

Anyway, George's misadventures in Indianapolis will come to an end one way or another and he'll go back to doing what he does best, which is delivering a football like few others can. Bobby Layne couldn't throw a ball like George (of course, George couldn't drink like Bobby Layne or Kenny Stabler or probably even Y.A. Tittle for that matter). Of course, Bobby Layne is in the Hall of Fame, while George and his card prices are in limbo or Indianapolis or both.

It's a perfect time to buy George. Sure, he's a gamble, but if you think *he's* a gamble, ask about Chris Webber. It's simple: George has the tools, and wherever he is they are going to have him throw the ball because he's too talented, too expensive and too much of a pain in the body parts to have him sitting around complaining. That means he'll put up some big numbers somewhere or get killed by some defensive lineman because he wasn't smart enough to realize that guys like Will Wolford are the ticket to good health and the Pro Football Hall of Fame. Either way, people will remember Jeff George and that's worth money, and probably a good deal more than his cards cost today.

59

Buy Alexei Kovalev.

Okay, so Alexei Kovalev doesn't
play defense. In fact, he leaves
that to the Red Army (he's not the first
player ever to do that), but in Kovalev
there's a hint of greatness that just
won't go away.

Remember, Kovalev is young, which gives him about 15 years to realize that moment in Game Seven of the Cup finals where he fakes out an entire team to score the winning goal, giving the Rangers their first championship since Franklin Roosevelt. Sure, it's a dream, but this kid has the talent, and if he listens to the likes of Messier maybe some day he can realize the promise.

If he does—and that's a big "if"—and does it in a Ranger jersey, his cards might just go straight through the Madison Square Garden roof and never return to earth. Even if he does it for someone else, he's still a human highlight film on skates, and at today's prices he's worth the gamble.

60

Buy Eric Lindros.

It's all too perfect. A Jeff George on skates. All the talent in the world. Maybe enough talent to revolutionize the game, but a head that makes general managers wince—plus he gets injured.

See Eric Lindros, see his card prices plummet, see people go broke selling Lindros to buy Alexandre Daigle. Forget Daigle, forget Kariya, forget Pronger, Lindros has already proven he can play and do it at an All-Star level.

Project Lindros over a whole season, see Lindros healthy, see Lindros with more support around him and what do you see? Don't kid yourself—you see NHL greatness, that's what you see, and all the moaning about his attitude and other problems doesn't change that fact one bit.

Lindros cards went up way too fast. The fact is he was the very first hockey rookie sensation, as by the time anyone outside of Canada discovered hockey cards Gretzky was old news and Lemieux was a hobbled poor man's version of the Great One. There have been no real hockey rookie sensations until now—nor was there ever anything close to a network hockey deal. That all changed with Lindros. He is the standard bearer of the new age of hockey and hockey cards.

Yes, he was way too expensive both in the flesh and on cardboard, but the prices on the cardboard went down while he waited to find a team he was willing to play on. Now that's done, and for a very brief moment people can be talked down on Lindros prices. Do it, because Lindros is for real.

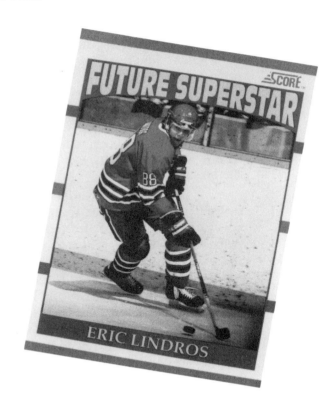

61

Buy Penguins.

What next? Zoo and barnyard animals? Maybe. The solid pick here is to buy Penguins. No, not the kind with wings, but rather the kind that came perilously close to that most dreaded of all things—a threepeat. Sure, they fell short, which tends to mean a softening if not an outright decline in prices.

If their loss means a decline, doesn't that mean that their two previous world championships pushed prices up? Of course, but it also means there are some darn fine players pretending to be penguins in Pittsburgh.

Everyone knows about Lemieux, who is now about a lock for the Hall of Fame, but there are others as well and they shouldn't be overlooked. Guys like Kevin Stevens and Jaromir Jagr are legitimate stars and there are a lot of other solid players as well.

You can never go too far wrong by getting in on a dynasty. Although the Penguins lost one, if their health holds out they should be around for years, which could mean a few more Stanley Cups and additional plus signs by their card prices.

62

Buy Don Mattingly cards.

For a while there, Don Mattingly was the card market. In 1984 he burst on the scene, and Donruss short-printed its run of baseball cards. That combination triggered a card-price hillclimb the likes of which we'll never see again. (Maybe. As Chuck Berry was fond of saying when he wasn't transporting underage women across state lines, "C'est la vie, say the old folks, it goes to show you never can tell," which has no direct bearing on this conversation but is nonetheless the chorus to a bitchin' song.) Mattingly was the perfect guy to start a card boom: He was from New York, he played first base and he hit home runs. Fans loved him, and he spoiled them with a run of seasons that just seemed to get better and better, and the card market hummed along and everything was so cozy and copacetic it made Constant Reader want to throw up.

Fortunately, nothing goes up forever, not Don Mattingly's seasons nor prices in the baseball-card market nor Constant Reader's dinner. Mattingly's Donruss rookie cards flirted with the $100 mark ever so briefly before sliding back down to around $40-$50, where they remain.

Geez; only $40-$50 for a Mattingly rookie? You'd think the guy wasn't getting in to the Hall of Fame or something.

Not to worry. Don Mattingly is a Hall of Famer. If he retired tomorrow he'd be a Hall of Famer just on the strength of what he's already done. Granted, he'll never be the hitter he was in his first couple of seasons in the League, when he was that rare combination of batting average and power that separates the Cooperstownies from the also-rans, but he's still capable of hitting .300 with 20 homers, and that's plenty. Throw that in on top of what Mattingly's already done and you've got frosting on a Cooperstown cake.

Listen: Don Mattingly's rookie card is cheaper than Joe Carter's rookie card. It's cheaper than Wade Boggs's rookie, Tony Gwynn's rookie and Ryne Sandberg's rookie—yet Mattingly still plays first base in New York and remains a favorite of Yankee fans. There is absolutely no reason not to buy his cards in quantity as soon as you possibly can. Buy his Donruss rookie first, and then follow with his Topps and Fleer rookies, his Topps Tiffany rookie, his Nestle's rookie, and then all his second-year cards. The cards are all undervalued and remain a prime example of the roller-coaster theory in action: The higher up they go, the farther they fall.

63

Hold Frank Thomas cards.

We interrupt this long string of buy recommendations for something of a warning: You won't make any money on Frank Thomas cards if you buy them now. It's definitely not a buyer's market if Frank Thomas is the player you want to buy. On the other hand, it's not really time to sell. All indications are that Frank Thomas can do better, that he has not hit the wall or the ceiling, that there is more there and more to come. He is such an unusual hitter, able to hit for power and hit for average, crank the ball out of the park or take a walk if need be, that he is one of the few players whom we feel comfortable in calling a sure thing, a certain Hall of Famer, at this very early stage in his career. Bill James's career projections, done in early 1993 for *Baseball America* (yet another reason to subscribe to this magazine as soon as your dogs can carry you to the phone), were merely the last piece of evidence we were looking for before we laid ourselves prostrate in front of Big Frank. O Most High Swami Bill figures that Thomas will play 19 years and hit .311 with 3,138 hits, 475 homers, 1,861 RBI, and 2,658 walks. Look at those numbers and tell me if those aren't Hall of Fame numbers—and not little Hall of Fame numbers, either. You know who has numbers that compare best with Frank Thomas? Willie Mays. Mays stole more bases and played an incredible center field, but Thomas is on a pace to walk more. And other than those disparities, everything else checks out.

Given that level of projected performance, a lot of Frank Thomas's cards aren't as expensive as they ought to be. His '90 Leaf card is, but other cards from that era aren't. His first Topps, Topps Tiffany, Score and Fleer cards aren't; neither is Frank's first Bowman card, his Bowman Tiffany, his Chicago White Sox team-issued card, his minor-league cards, or any of a myriad of cards from Thomas's young career.

It's conceivable that Thomas could become another Nolan Ryan, so that recommendation to hold Frank Thomas really ought to be a recommendation to buy Frank Thomas—but buy Frank Thomas judiciously. Stay away from the well-publicized items and really become a Frank Thomas collector. Go after the little-known items— the team-issued cards, the food issues—that are likely to be in demand several years from now, when Thomas is really all the rage and the mainline Thomas items are being priced out of collectors' price ranges. What's more, you're likely to find that becoming a Frank Thomas collector is—dare we say it?—fun. Parents, this is something you can do with your kids. Non-parents, this is a great way to learn about a lot of card issues you may have never known previously existed.

Here's how we would go about putting together a Frank Thomas collection: First, we'd have our computer software search out all the cards it has in its database; this is one area where the Card Collector software really shines. Next, we'd grab our copy of *The Standard Catalog of Baseball Cards* (Krause Publications, $29.95; if you don't have a copy to grab, chances are your local library will) to fill in the miscellaneous issues that aren't in the database. Then we'd go out to shows and stores and hunt down Frank Thomas cards. The nice thing about buying some of the miscellaneous cards you'll be hunting down is that a lot of dealers don't have any idea what some of the cards are and what their real worth is. I mean, do you know what's rarer: A Mootown Snackers Thomas card or a Cracker Jack four-in-one featuring Thomas? (Answer: The Cracker Jack four-in-one, by a nose.) Not only will you come away from the whole thing a more tightly-knit family and money ahead to boot, but you'll be better-informed collector/investors for it.

Maybe you didn't think so much could be involved in a simple recommendation to hold onto your Frank Thomas cards. Well, everything in this business is simple, but the simple stuff is a lot more complex than it seems. Which is why we recommend, among other things, that you...

64

Buy Barry Bonds cards.

Barry Bonds doesn't get more respect from card collector/investors for a very simple reason: He acts like a jerk. While this impression can be overcome through the sheer weight of numbers—e.g., Rickey Henderson—it doesn't do wonders for the image of a player or the value of his cards over the long term.

Unfortunately, players change from being nice guys to being doorknobs at the drop of a $24 million contract, so there's no telling who will be the next peach among men to turn into skunk droppings. Willie Mays has already turned hindquarters-front; Jose Canseco wavers between handsome prince and prince of darkness. The next one to turn tail might be Frank Thomas or Ken Griffey Jr. or Cal Ripken Jr.; no one knows. The only thing certain is that when he does, duck; otherwise his cards will konk you on the head on their way down.

By the same token, Barry Bonds

could mellow as maturity approaches, just like...uh, just like a baseball player could conceivably do, given the proper astrological collisions and a stiff shot of sodium pentothal. If that happened, prices for Barry Bonds cards would skyrocket as collectors realized that by golly, he is the best player in baseball after all.

Bonds is the best player in baseball, and the prices of his cards don't reflect it. Hey, $15 max for one of his rookie cards? (That number may be seriously out of date by the time this actually reaches your hands, but take our word for it—this card is priced at $15 in August 1993.) That's ridiculous! Joe Carter rookies are four times that, and Joe Carter is one-quarter the player Barry Bonds is.

Take our word for it: Buy all the early Barry Bonds cards you can. We especially like the 1987 Fleer Glossy Tin version of the Bonds cards. These shiny beauties go for about the same as the regular Fleer versions and are at least half as plentiful. The '88s and '89s are even scarcer and should be snapped up immediately if you get the chance.

Again, Barry Bonds's reputation for being a sour-puss is working against him right now. But there are so many sourpusses and potential sourpusses in baseball right now who don't have a grain of the talent Bonds has that you have to figure at some point the cursing will cease and the serious buying will begin.

Or Barry Bonds could suddenly turn into a nice guy.
On second thought...nah.

65

Buy Jose Canseco cards.

This one is Kit's idea, and it's probably come from the same spot in his brain that commanded, "Buy Bob Hamelin cards."

On the other hand, it's not the worst idea ever offered up for ritual sacrifice. Canseco rookies are $50 and dropping fast. (By the time this is published, it's conceivable that they could be selling for $30-$35.) If Jose Canseco does anything at all with the rest of his career—and granted, that's an "if" the size of Antarctica—he'll go into the Hall of Fame. He already has almost 250 home runs, and he's young enough (29) and talented enough to hit 250 more.

Canseco is at a crossroads. If he takes the low road and goofs around with his career and lets the fire for baseball flicker and die, he'll be another Darryl Strawberry—all the talent in the world and none of the stuff that goes with it. On the other hand, if he takes the high road, he'll get to

Scotland before ye. NO! If he takes the high road and revives his desire to play and shows the intensity he must have shown at one point in his career, his cards will shoot back up and everyone, including Jose, will be happy.

Canseco presents you with a dilemma not unlike that faced by Jabez Stone in *The Devil and Daniel Webster*. Do you resist falling for the buy-Jose-Canseco-card pitch and walk the upright and God-fearing way the rest of your days, or do you let the guy with the pointy shoes and the filed teeth prick your finger? We say—or rather, Kit says—let him prick.

66

Buy Larry Walker cards.

Montreal is such a wonderful place it's hard sometimes to understand why so few players want to play there. Maybe it's the fact that everyone in Montreal speaks French and acts cosmopolitan, and neither of these behaviors (behaviors, *s'il vous plait*) are normally associated with baseball players. Maybe it's the fact that baseball in Montreal exists merely to keep the real hardcore sports fans occupied between hockey seasons. Maybe it's because Montreal is Canadian and baseball is American, though this hasn't proven to be too much of a hindrance to Toronto.

Whatever the reason, it's forced Montreal to develop one of the best minor-league systems in baseball. If it's not going to be able to keep its players past the time when they're eligible for free agency or attract top-name, big-dollar free agents, then Montreal darn well had better be able to get the best possible players through its system and up to the big club while they're still

Expo property. That's one of the reasons why the Expos play baseball the way a five-year-old paints: boldly, colorfully, but without a lot of execution and polish.

Which reminds us of Larry Walker. Walker is one of the greatest baseball stories you'll ever find. He grew up outside of Vancouver and, like most creatures who grow up outside of Vancouver, was a hockey player. He used baseball to keep himself occupied between hockey seasons. One day he was playing sandlot ball in a primitive British Columbian sandlot league when a scout spotted him and saw something. It could have been the 70mm-howitzer arm. It could have been the speed on the bases and the instinct in the outfield. It could have been the quick left-handed bat. Whatever it was, it convinced the scout that this guy was going to be a player, and more than that, the perfect player for Montreal. So the Expos signed him and set about the task of turning him into a baseball player.

It took a few years, including one wasted year of surgery and rehabilitation after a catcher performed knee surgery on Walker during a collision at home plate. But now Walker is at or near the top of the league in most offensive categories, and there is absolutely no reason why he cannot continue to just improve and improve and improve.

Because Walker plays in Canada his cards aren't all that expensive. Outside of his Leaf card (which is a silly $14) Walker's rookie cards are 60¢ to 75¢. There are a few odd limited-edition inserts, most notably a Donruss Elite card and a ToppsBlackGold card, which tip the scales a little with Walker, but basically all of Walker's cards are cheap and not going up in value at the same rate at which he continues to improve.

If the sole criterion for buying the cards of any player who isn't a rookie is Hall-of-Fame worthiness, then Walker might come up a little bit short. But fortunately Hall-of-Fame worthiness isn't always the sole criterion. There's also value to consider. Are a player's cards undervalued in relation to his level of performance and likely to go up soon? The answer for Walker is yes. And that makes him a buy.

67

Buy Juan Gonzalez cards.

Our friend Greg Ambrosius, erstwhile editor of *Fantasy Baseball* and SCD On-Line and the author of the investment column for *Sports-Cards-formerly-Baseball-Cards* magazine, is a wonderful and talented guy except for one small personality flaw: He plays basketball the same way Dick Butkus played linebacker. Okay, Greg Ambrosius is a wonderful and talented guy except for two small personality flaws: He plays basketball the way Dick Butkus played linebacker, and he believes that he discovered Juan Gonzalez. Nary an investment column or an issue of *Fantasy Baseball* goes by—still—without Greg plugging Juan Gonzalez as the Next Big Thing, and it gives you a big forearm shiver to the face if you don't just drop everything and get this guy's cards now and get this guy on your fantasy team, because Greg Ambrosius is dead-set convinced that Juan Gonzalez is the gen-you-whine article, a guy whose future is, as

Greg is fond of saying, ahead of him.

Turns out Greg is right, but there are lots of people who were onto Juan Gonzalez while Greg Ambrosius was still writing girls' hoops stories in Baraboo, Wisconsin. Gonzalez signed with the Rangers when he was 16 and took his time winding his way through the Rangers organization along with fellow 16-year-old signee Sammy Sosa. Along the way his numbers weren't great and he had little power at all to start with, but when you realized that Gonzalez was four or five years younger than the people he was playing with and holding his own, you sat up and took notice. And then when the power did come and Juan Gonzalez began to discover things like the wonders of weightlifting and how to lay off the big two-strike breaking ball, you really took notice. Now Gonzalez is a complete package—and he's still so goldarn young you have to shake your head at what he's done already and make some scary projections for his future.

Because of all the amazing things Juan Gonzalez has been doing lately his cards have moved up in value, but they're still real cheap based on Gonzalez' age and accomplishments. A particular favorite is the reversed-negative Gonzalez rookie card from the 1990 Donruss set. Granted, anything from '90 Donruss tends to roll over and play dead, but the reversed-negative rookie is about the only exception. It was undervalued to start with, and now at $4—four freaking dollars!!?!??!—it's a total steal. Neglect all the Leaf stuff and the Stadium Club stuff and the Ultra stuff and the Upper Deck stuff and jump on this card (though you might want to put it in a rigid card holder before you jump on it too roughly).

Actually, our previous comments on Juan Gonzalez may have been a little too harsh. We think you should jump on anything from the early stages of Juan Gonzalez's career, including Leaf, Stadium Club, Ultra, and minor-league cards, of which there are a lot because of the time Gonzalez spent working his way up to the bigs. Again, put them in rigid plastic holders before you do any serious jumping on them. Better safe than sorry.

68

Buy Gregg Jefferies cards.

This one's wonderful because it's so darn perverse. Gregg Jefferies was the new savior of the baseball-card market when he arrived on the scene in 1988. He was the Mets' version of Don Mattingly: white, and a natural hitter to boot. (Or maybe it's a natural hitter, and white besides. But his two distinguishing attributes were definitely that he was white and he could hit.) Unfortunately, there were far too many Jefferies cards made—he was even a double-print in the Donruss set that year—Jefferies wasn't an instant success, and the market for his cards went south about as quickly as a hijacked jetliner, and took the Donruss set and a good chunk of the rest of the card market with him.

But the funny thing is Jefferies doesn't have a bad career by any means up to this date, and he may even have a Hall of Fame career put together by the time all is said and done. He's never hit worse than the high .270s, with good power, runs batted in and speed. He's only 26-going-on-27, so there's lots more where that came from. And he got such an early start on things that he could really do something by the time his career winds up.

And his cards are so darn cheap, too. You can get the prime Gregg Jefferies cards for $1.75 according to the price guides but a lot less than that in reality. Make a lot of dealers an offer and you can have whatever Jefferies cards you want in whatever quantities they have on hand. This is especially true in New York, where Jefferies is afforded the same hale welcome as Bobby Bonilla or Vince Coleman.

At $1.75 and lower, Jefferies cards are something you can make money on. Okay, so the guy isn't going into the Hall of Fame and may never measure up to the expectations that were set for him. But that's certainly not his fault, and over the short term at least it shouldn't be considered a strike against his cards.

69

Buy Cliff Floyd cards.

The major-league baseball-card makers are quite a bit like the old Greek gods, in the sense that they spend most of their time screwing things up for the lumpenproles, screwing each other and then turning themselves into farm animals.

In the case of rookie cards the Greek gods really screwed things up big-time. Instead of the logical system of days gone by, when players would play or very, very nearly play and get a major-league card in return, starting in approximately 1991 the Big Five card-makers thought it would make sense to make major-league cards of every player who stood even an outside chance of making it to the big leagues, under the assumption that if Bing Schwing actually did make it to the big leagues there would be a sudden push for Der Bingle's cards, and the only set that would have them would be...actually, everyone's, since there wasn't much scooping that ever took place from one set to the other. The players one set had, everyone had, and the players one set missed (Jeff Bagwell and Pat Listach, for instance), everyone missed.

The primary result of this relentless search for the Next Big Thing has been a shift in focus from the majors to the minors for the card buyer looking to cash in on the next sensation. Fortunately, there are enough Next Big Things floating around the minor league to make things interesting, to say the least. Some of these things have made it up to the majors. But enough remain in the minors priced at minor-league prices to make you want to abandon the relative security of major-league sets and look at some hot minor-league players as places to stash your money.

Floyd is our personal favorite. Imagine a player with the sock of Willie McCovey and the speed to play center field and you have Cliff Floyd. He's annihilated pitching everywhere he's been, and he's just about ready for the majors. Naturally, because Floyd hasn't played a game in the major leagues he has about 15 major-league cards ranging in price from 40¢ to $10. The basic cards, his Topps card, his Bowman card and minor-league cards from Fleer and Upper Deck, are the ones to buy out of this mess. They cost less to buy and stand a better chance of doubling or tripling in value—which seems pretty likely, given all the damage Floyd is capable of wreaking. Willie McCovey with speed...quite a thought, isn't it?

Buy Jeffrey Hammonds cards.

Hammonds is a nicer version of Barry Bonds with every last one of Bonds's tools. He came out of college acknowledged to be the best player in the draft, and he fell from the very tippy-top only because he had the reputation of being unsignable. Hammonds cards aren't selling for quite what Bonds' cards are, though you can't touch anything of Hammonds's for less than a buck. In fact, the only Hammonds card that you could call rationally priced is his '92 Topps Traded card, which shows him in his Team USA uniform. Focus on them, buy them, but be prepared to hold them for just a little while until you can double your money. That day will come within the next 18 months—Hammonds is a very sure thing, hence the high entry fee for his cards—and you will do well with any Jeffrey Hammonds cards you buy. But because of the high initial cost, Hammonds cards should not be the centerpiece of your portfolio.

Buy Manny Ramirez cards.

Every so often you find a player you know is special, and as you follow him through the minor leagues he does nothing to alter your opinion of him, and then when he finally hits the bigs he does it in such a way that you feel vindicated, as if all the time you spent plotting his upward curve to the major had some sort of bearing on his career. Ken Griffey Jr. was a player like that. So were Frank Thomas, Barry Bonds and Juan Gonzalez. And so is Manny Ramirez.

Ramirez ought to be a basketball story. He played his way off of New York's mean streets and found the fame and security and fortune that goes with being a No. 1 draft pick by the Indians. He idolizes Roberto Clemente and plays the game with the same elan and intensity. He has played better and better as he has moved up through the Indians' system. He is almost ready, and he may be in the majors by the time you read this.

Just on the face of it Ramirez is a better buy than Jeffrey Hammonds. Ramirez's cards are in the 25¢-75¢ range, with only a few special cards booking for more than a dollar. His draft-pick cards in the regular '92 Bowman, Pinnacle and Upper Deck sets are personal favorites. Sure, Ramirez may be just another Cleveland hitter, but if you believe as we do that the Indians have a groovy thing going with their young hitters, then it behooves you to jump on Ramirez with both feet.

It will be much easier for you to double your money on Manny Ramirez than on Jeffrey Hammonds. That in and of itself is not the reason to buy Ramirez's cards. The ability of his cards to serve as a short-term turnaround investment or a long-term buy is.

72

Buyest thou not cards of young pitchers.

This was going to be a series of rhyming Elizabethan couplets that would gently mock Shakesperean verse while reminding you that it's not a good idea to buy cards of young pitchers as they move up through the minor leagues, but once we realized that would be a really stupid idea we gave it up and returned once more to English prose, where we would like to remind you:

For crumb's sake, lay off the goldarn pitcher cards, willya?

It's not that we don't have a world of admiration for Todd Van Poppel and Brien Taylor and Steve Karsay and Aaron Sele and Paul Spojlaric or however you spell his name; it's just that we think that as card buys they're not worth the headaches they can cause.

Take Van Poppel. He was the most heralded draft pick since Ken Griffey Jr. The Braves laid off of him because they thought he was unsignable (there's a thought for you, huh: Todd Van Poppel in a Braves rotation that already has two Cy Young winners plus John Smoltz and Steve Avery) but the A's opened their wallets to prove that anything was possible with the application of enough money. Van Poppel nudged his way up through the A's farm system, and when Frank Thomas was crushing homers at the big-league level, Van Poppel was still in A ball, struggling with his control. Van Poppel was shut down a couple of times because of arm trouble but is a big-league pitcher now, however tentatively. He may be a 20-game winner, he may not be. But for a guy with so much buildup and hype, and the card values to match, there's not much there.

Same with Brien Taylor. He came out of high school almost as hyped as Van Poppel, and who knows? He may be the next great pitcher in baseball. But he has so much farther to go than a comparable hitter would that you have to say he probably won't make it as big as most people are saying and a lot of card buyers are hoping.

The problem is that most young pitchers are drafted on their ability to throw a fastball. The harder they throw, the higher they go. Breaking balls and control and holding runners on and throwing the right pitch in the right situation come later—only sometimes they come and sometimes they don't. And if they do come, sometimes the fastballs go as recompense. Hitters usually have more facets to their game when they get drafted and less to go wrong once they get into the system.

The message here is that you'll spend about the same buying cards of minor-league-phenom pitchers as you will buying cards of their counterpart hitters, so you might as well buy the cards of the hitters. They're easier to predict, they'll make the majors more quickly, and it's easier to make money on them. In other words,

"Should wildness come and impert'ly steal
Thy gifts from thee and leave thee low:
Know'st thou soft the way I feel:
Hitters are the way to go."
Or the modern colloquial equivalent.

73

Avoid Atlanta Braves prospects. And if you've got 'em, sell 'em.

We don't have anything against Chipper Jones or Ryan Klesko or Mike Kelly or Javy Lopez or Tony Tarasco or Jose Oliva or current San Diego Padre Marvin Nieves as players or human beings or anything. We just don't think they're going to be players whose real worth will be matched by the worth of their cards right now.

Chipper Jones was the butt of everyone's jokes when the Braves passed over Todd Van Poppel to draft the high-school shortstop No. 1 overall in the 1989 draft. But Jones proved the critics wrong by improving his bat and working on his defense. Now Jones looks like the more complete prospect—pitchers will do it to you every time—and the better potential major-leaguer.

Jones looks like a good major-leaguer, all right, but good in the sense of being another Travis Fryman, not another Cal Ripken Jr. Jones will be a solid power hitter and a good average hitter for a lot of years, but he will not be a Hall of Famer. You can take that to the bank.

Klesko, meanwhile, was a pitcher with a torn-out rotator cuff who was taken by the Braves as a hitter and has turned into a heck of a hitter. In the minors Klesko has been able to hit for both average and power; in the majors only the power is likely to remain.

Kelly, much like Barry Bonds, was the college player of the year at Arizona State but has not shown the sort of development in the minors the Braves were expecting. The power is there, but Kelly hits for a lousy average and strikes out far too much for a hitter who was supposedly polished.

The rest of the prospects in the Braves' organization, or prospects who were in the Braves' organization but were traded away, aren't much. Tarasco is a singles hitter; Nieves, who was dealt to the Padres in the Fred McGriff deal, is the second coming of Geronimo Berroa; Lopez will be eaten alive offensively by the strain of having to catch every day; and Oliva has a long way to come before he amounts to anything.

The prices for Jones, Kelly and Klesko cards are all over the place, but the important ones cost more than a buck. You'll never make any kind of decent money on Jones, Kelly and Klesko cards starting from that high platform. And as long as the Braves keep playing to a national-television audience that platform is going to remain high.

You can get decent money for cards of Jones, Kelly and Klesko if you dump them now. Settle for decent money. Dump them now.

74

Buy David McCarty cards.

The parallels between David McCarty and Mark McGwire are sweet. Both were outstanding hitters in the Pac-10, and both have last names that start with "Mc." Isn't that sweet?

But actually, McCarty has the potential to be much greater than McGwire. His ability to hit for average is better, and unlike Mike Kelly, McCarty has found he can still hit for a high average in the minor leagues without sacrificing power.

McCarty can play first base or the outfield but is likely to play first base in Minnesota, replacing Kent "Shamu" Hrbek. Shamu isn't ready to waddle off to a blissful retirement at Sea World just yet, though, so McCarty has to bide his time in the minors, play every day and wait for the occasional callup. He showed a lot in his mid-season-'93 promotion but the rest of the team didn't, so his boxscores tended to get lost.

That won't last. McCarty is a

superb hitting prospect and is worth the buck or so you'll have to pay for his cards. (Here's a tip for you: Wait until the off-season and try to negotiate dealers down for their McCarty cards. As long as you're not in the Upper Midwest you should be able to get some buys.) His first major-league card is a highly doctored, computer-tricked-over beauty in the '91 Upper Deck set (No. 75) and should be the focus of most of your buying efforts. You can make money over both the short term and the long term with David McCarty cards, and you can make deals right now. Go do it.

75

Buy Chad Mottola cards.

Now we're getting down there. Mottola was the top pick of the Reds in the '92 draft, and the boy is a hitter. He was an awesome hitter in college—the University of Central Florida—and has been a minor-league terror so far. He is going to go through the minors fast and get to the big leagues in a hurry, and he'll make an impact once he gets there.

Mottola's best card so far is a draft-pick card in the '93 Topps set. You can buy the regular one in quantity for around 50¢ a card, but try to splurge on a couple of the ToppsGold cards if you can.

Fifty cents is actually quite a lot to spend on a player whose major-league debut is likely several years away (though expansion has changed all that; players are now rushing through the minors and coming up to the majors faster than ever before, and prospects you thought were two years away are suddenly THERE). Try to bargain down on Mottola cards; you should be able to do it. But if you have to pay 50¢ for Chad Mottola cards, so be it. The guy's worth it.

76

Buy Michael Tucker cards.

Buying cards of infielders is usually a no-no because too often the hyped infielder turns out to be Chuck Knoblauch or Walt Weiss. In the case of Michael Tucker, we think we can make an exception.

Tucker is a package: Speed and power, and batting average besides. He came out of a very small college in Virginia, so he was something of an unknown quantity coming into the big leagues, even though he did shine with Team USA. It was initially thought that Tucker was too good a hitter to play shortstop or second base, but this has not been so. Tucker has shown he could play an adequate major-league second base, and has kept hitting all along.

Tucker cards are a prohibitive $3 in the '92 Bowman set but a much more affordable 50¢ in the '92 Topps Traded set. Pick up as many of the Topps Traded singles as you can—or, hey, go for the set, which gives you

Jeffrey Hammonds and Tucker and Phil Nevin and Darren Dreifort and Charles Johnson and Calvin Murray for around $15 a pop.

Tucker is the guy who is going to supplant Roberto Alomar as the No. 1 offensive infielder in baseball. And he's going to do it soon.

77

Buy Johnny Damon cards.

Johnny Damon is not some '50s rocker from the Italian part of Philly who sang one teenage death song, made it to *American Bandstand*, dated Little Peggy March, and now spends his golden years touring with Lou Christie and Sgt. Barry Sadler. Damon is an outfielder in the Royals' chain who was the best hitter anywhere in any sort of baseball the year before he was eligible to be drafted but only hit .305 the year of the draft and slipped into the second round, where the Royals grabbed him without hesitation.

Damon is going to be a fantastic major-league hitter. His cards are cheap now, especially compared to the Jeffrey Hammonds and Michael Tuckers of the world. His sole '92 minor-league card is in the Upper Deck minor-league set, and lists for a quarter. A quarter? A QUARTER??? Go get it. Buy it. Snarf it up. Inhale it whole. Get it into your portfolio and hang onto it like it was gold. Johnny Damon represents a rare opportunity in these days of rookie cards and pre-pre-rookie cards and out-and-out hype crap like '92 Bowman to buy one solitary card of a young player and watch it go up in value. Do it. It'll be fun.

78

Sell your Frankie Rodriguez cards.

Hey, we're former journalists forced into this line of work because of gambling debts and poor investments; we know a good story when we see one. And Frankie Rodriguez was a great story.

Imagine a guy who could play shortstop on your team and hit .400 with twenty-some home runs. Then imagine that when he wasn't playing short he could pitch, and throw 98-mile-an-hour fastballs past anyone. And then imagine that he was drafted but didn't sign until the 59th minute of the 11th hour. That was Frankie Rodriguez.

Rodriguez was playing junior-college ball in San Jacinto, Texas, when he did all this. The Red Sox drafted Rodriguez as a "draft-and-follow" player, meaning they had one year after he was drafted to sign him up. The Red Sox took all of that year, signing Rodriguez just as the deadline was about to expire. Just like that he was in the minors and Upper Deck had him in its Final Edition set and the world was Frankie Rodriguez crazy.

Well, the craze is over, the dust has settled, and it appears as though Rodriguez will be a major-league closer. Big deal. Major-league closers do not deserve $1.25 minor-league cards, and the system will not support $1.25 minor-league cards for major-league closers. Sell your Frankie Rodriguez cards, particularly the Upper Deck Final Edition Rodriguez, and console yourself with the knowledge that, boy, you were right on top of that story.

Just like *Inside Edition*.

79

At least consider buying some 1989-91 Bowman sets.

We will admit that we loathe the revived Bowman cards. We despise '89-'91 Bowman, and we consider '92 Bowman to be a monument to stupidity and greed in the card market, so maybe we're not the best people to make recommendations on Bowman cards. It's just that the original Bowmans were so good and so true to their admittedly low purpose that we couldn't tolerate the bargain-basement fit and finish Topps applied to the cards it called Bowmans when it resurrected the name in 1989. The photos on the card fronts were nasty, the print job was horrible, the backs were musty, the stats were unintelligible, the size of the first set was incompatible with any plastic sheet on the market, and Topps compounded things by making so many Bowmans that mass-market stores like Kmart began strapping boxes of it to the feet of its shorter salesclerks so their heads could poke up above the counter.

With all those nasty words said, in the light of hindsight the stuff doesn't look nearly so bad—as an investment, mind you. The thinking behind the stuff still makes our skin crawl. It's chock-full of rookies and draft picks and phenoms and prospects and out-and-out minor-league scrubeenies, and its non-designed designs look a lot better than some of the designed designs that came out of the era. (Donruss comes instantly to mind.) Overproduction is still a concern, but so much Bowman was returned and destroyed that it's actually out in less quantity than comparable sets.

It's affordable, too. The '89, '90 and '91 sets together can be had for less than $50, or one-quarter of the cost of the '92 set alone. There's a disparity between the products, but not that much of disparity. And the way this market works, a lot of people who feel they missed out on '92 Bowman will be coming back for the older stuff before too long.

Bowman represents everything that's bad about the baseball-card market. So you should probably have some around.

80

Buy Topps Bigs.

We have a very warm place in our heart for Topps Big cards because they're everything that Bowmans are not. They're a quality card, true to the original spirit of Topps. Topps began making these in 1988 as a sort of updated version of and tribute to the '55 Topps cards. The cards were the size of the '55s, they were horizontal, they used graphics that reminded you of the '55s without ripping them off explicitly, they were issued in three series, and they came out during the summer, when kids were around to buy them.

The idea took off like gangbusters, but by the time the third series rolled around all the problems of the old '55s came back to haunt the Bigs— namely, no one gives a rip about the last series of anything when there's more than two series of it.

Topps gamely stuck with the Big idea for two more years, making less and less of the product each go-round, so that by the time it came to the last series of the last year the product was genuinely scarce.

Topps Bigs are fun to collect and cheap. Wax boxes will run you less than $10 per, and the pricing hasn't come around to reflect the scarcity of the series. Everything's about the same price regardless.

As a collector you should have all three sets. As an investor you should focus on the last series of '89 and the entire '90 series (which also features members of the 1990 U.S. Olympic Baseball Team). Buy it when you see it and hang onto it; it's cheap, and its day is coming.

It's hard to say exactly when the renaissance will come for Topps Bigs. The cards are a contrary investment right now and haven't shown any signs of catching fire in the six months or so we've been recommending them to buyers. We may just be letting our sentimentality get in the way of our judgment with these cards. But we also know that our feelings for these cards are not unique. Other people share them. And as long as that's the case, these cards are worth buying.

81

Buy stickers.

This opinion is not shared by anyone the authors know of but is the result of their many years of experience in this market and related markets and several nights of heavy drinking.

The basis behind recommending stickers as a buy is this: In other fields, the most valuable collectibles that were once available to the public at large are those that were meant to be used up and were essentially destroyed when used. Unassembled model kits. Unpunched punch-out books. A piece of Joe DiMaggio's wedding cake.

(This particular item showed up in a Leland's auction several years ago and boggled the minds of more than one person who saw it listed in the catalog. First of all, who would go to Joe D's wedding, get a piece of cake, and not eat it? And if they didn't eat it, why didn't they just throw it out instead of saving it all those years? And if they didn't eat it and did save it, why didn't they get Joe D to sign it, or at least throw in an unopened Mr. Coffee to go along with it? Sheesh, some people.)

Anyhow, the way you use a sticker is to stick it on something—good furniture, usually. When you do that its collectability is ruined, and someone is really ticked off. And the people who bought stickers tended to stick them on things.

As a result you don't see many stickers for sale. Single stickers? Forget it. You can find an occasional dealer with a bunch of unopened packs and boxes he's willing to dump, but because so much of this product went to conventional retailers and was either sold or destroyed, you're not going to cherrypick rookies out of a stack of stickers.

That's the bad news. The good news is that when you find stickers their prices are almost always reasonable. The fact that they're scarce doesn't figure into the equation when stickers are priced; many dealers who have stickers go by the price guides with them, and the few price guides that list stickers put the most expensive set at $20.

They're worth more than that. The sets to go after from strictly a card-collectors' standpoint are the card-sized Fleer Star Stickers, which were issued in 1981 and again in 1987 and '88. They're really attractive and carry the same information on their backs that the baseball cards do. The 1989 Topps Stickercards are also a novel concept—a card of one player on one side and a sticker of a different player on the other. There are a myriad of sticker and card combinations, and a combination of superstar card and superstar sticker ought to bring good money but doesn't.

The rest of the sticker sets are scarcer because they look like they were meant to be stuck, and they also have the drawback of looking less like cards than the Star Stickers and Stickercards. The most interesting set of the bunch is the '87 Topps sticker set, which features two variations: a more common version that reads "Printed in Italy" on the back, and a scarcer "Printed in U.S.A." version. The two versions came about after Topps and Panini severed their relationship (for obvious reasons, Panini made its own set of stickers the next year) and Topps had to scramble to find a new printer.

Stickers, again, are a contrary investment. They don't cost much but they haven't paid off any so far. If you decide you want to stick a fair chunk of money into stickers, do it with the knowledge it could be some time before that money ever comes back out in quantity. Keep your eyes open, don't peel the backs, and you'll do fine.

82

Buy Topps Double-headers, 3-Ds, Tripleheaders, and other miscellaneous Topps.

Topps may look like a cardmaking company but it's really a candy company. It bleeds Gold Rush Bubble Gum and Thumb Fun Anatomically Correct Candy. It revels in Wacky Packages and Garbage Pail Kids. And it's hard for Topps to settle down and make nothing but Stadium Club cards and Bowman jumbos for the rest of its life.

That's why every now and then Topps likes to put out something from way out in left field on the market, just to see how it goes. Topps calls them "test issues," and the most successful test issues make it into regular production. Topps Kids cards were a test issue that made it (and provide a lot of yuks for little bucks); so were Topps Micro Baseball, a.k.a. Baseball Cards in A Tube. And so were Topps 3-Ds, Heads-Ups, Tripleheaders and Doubleheaders.

Topps 3-Ds looked as if they were made by that quintessential '70s kids' toy, the Mattel Vac-U-Form. You put a sheet of plastic and mold in the Vac-U-Form, pressed it together, added heat and—whammo!—out came something really useless. Topps 3-Ds were like that: a sheet of plastic Vac-U-Formed to the rough dimensions of the pictured player. Topps made these wonders in 1985 and '86 on a semi-test-issue basis, and, gee, wonder of wonders, never really sold them in any quantity. Despite that they're cheap; you might spend a buck or two on a Don Mattingly, but everyone else in the set is 50¢ or less.

Topps Heads-Ups were more of a test issue, and with good reason: They were ugly. They consisted of a huge player head with a suction cup on a swivel on the back, for mounting. That meant that not only could you take your Jose Canseco head with you practically anywhere and stick it on anything, but you could spin it round and round, too. These are more expensive—a couple of bucks each for the commons up to $10 for the big stars—but they are very scarce and definitely worth picking up when you have the chance.

Tripleheaders are plastic mini-baseballs with three bogus player signatures. They were a test issue in 1992 and can be found today in the hands of dealers who don't have the foggiest idea what they are. If you can find them for less than a buck each they're a good buy.

Doubleheaders were made by Topps in 1991 and consist of a mini-card of a player on one side, a mini-rookie-card of the same player on the other side, and creamy filling in the middle. No, actually they consist of a mini-card of a player on one side, a mini-rookie-card of the same player on the other side, and a plastic base. They cost about 75¢ each when they were released and can be found today for that or less. They're worth buying at about 50¢ each.

Going through Topps test issues is like going to a trash-and-treasure sale. It's usually more trash than treasure...but you just never know.

83

Buy Donruss Pop-Ups, Opening Day sets, and All-Stars.

Donruss's approach to cards was always less playful than Topps's, but that doesn't mean Donruss didn't uncork a wild pitch or two from time to time. In fact, through the mid-'80s Donruss was a regular Steve Dalkowski of the card business, throwing 'em back to the screen with alacrity. And funky borders.

Donruss really could crank 'em out then: Season Highlights. Hall of Fame Champions. Baseball's Best. Super Diamond Kings. And our favorites, Pop-Ups, Opening Day Sets, and All-Stars.

Donruss All-Stars were originally huge cards called Action All-Stars. They were sold in cellophane packs of three or four cards each and were terribly easy to cherry-pick, if you were so inclined. They didn't sell well, and when Donruss came to the hard conclusion that the reason they didn't sell well was the same reason Topps Giants didn't sell well all those years, and that was because they were TOO DARN BIG, Donruss downsized the cards and stuck them in packs with similarly downsized Donruss Pop-Ups. Today the five sets of oversized All-Stars (1983-87) and downsized All-Stars (1988) can be had for about $50, which is a good buy. They'll never make huge jumps in value but they will continue to go up, and the early sets have the added bonus of not only being something different but looking the part.

Pop-Ups were diecut cards that showed the starting lineups for each All-Star team. They were usually tall and thin and had the host stadium worked into the background. Donruss made them from 1986-88 and sold them with the All-Stars. They were good fun their first two years of production, but by 1988 everything was card-sized and dull, and the rummage-sale-in-a-pack effect the cards had previously had no longer meant much.

The Opening Day set was issued in 1987 and utilized the novel concept of showing everyone who was in the starting lineup for each major-league team on opening day. It was clever, so clever that Donruss made what seemed like 38.9 bazillion sets, enough sets for every man, woman and child in the world to have 4.7 sets apiece. Fortunately, on about one-tenth of one percent of the sets Donruss inserted a Barry Bonds card that showed a photo of Johnny Ray instead of Bonds. These cards are the most valuable errors of the modern card era—and they could still be out there, because so many dealers have never opened their sets.

You can find Opening Day sets for $10-$12. The Bonds card alone is a $500 item. Is it worth the gamble? We think so.

84

Buy Fleer boxed sets.

We never thought we would say it. For the longest time Kit Kiefer would get the laugh track rolling in the "New Stuff" section of *Baseball Cards* magazine by ripping on Fleer boxed sets. "Sputum on cardboard," he would call them, and for the six years of their existence (1985-90), they were. Fleer boxed sets feature some of the most hideous designs, silly player selections (David Cone a Hero of Baseball? Oil Can Boyd a Baseball All-Star?) and nasty photos this side of Donruss Triple Play cards. They were bad things, plain and simple, made on the cheap for various mass retailers so that they could have a card product none of the other mass retailers had, even if it was dreck and the other mass retailers actually had the same dreck in a different box.

And so they rolled out of the Mighty Fleer Bubble-Gum Factory and Dreck Machine: Baseball All-Stars, for Ben Franklin; Award Winners, for 7-

Eleven; Fleer Limited Edition, for Walgreens; Baseball's Exciting Stars, for Cumberland Farms; Record Setters, for Eckerd Drug; Superstars, for McCrory; and our personal favorite, Baseball's Best: Slugger's Vs. Pitchers, for McCrory, McClellan, J.J. Newberry, H.L. Green, and TG&Y stores.

(Many of these stores are bankrupt now, and based on the luck they had with the Baseball's Best set, not by accident.)

Many of the sets, especially the ones made for Walgreens, 7-Eleven, Kmart and Kay-Bee Toy, are still common as dirt and not worth buying. Sets made for Cumberland Farms and the McCrory chain are less common and do carry a smidgen of value, though not of the redeeming social type. However, dealers and price guides tend to lump all of them together and sell them for whatever the market will bear, which is usually $5-$6 each. They're worth more than that just for the single cards alone, and perhaps even more than that as unbroken sets somewhere down the road.

See, we have a theory about this stuff, which goes: Fleer is trying to make itself a household name, like Coca-Cola. It wants to be an international marketing company trading on its name as much as on its products. In the next several years we'll see Fleer jackets and caps and shirts and maybe even Fleer wallpaper, all designed to boost the image of Fleer. That will create a secondary wave of demand for anything Fleer, which will sweep up these sets and transport them to places they've never been. Like $10 a set.

The sets we recommend are: any of the Baseball's Best: Sluggers Vs. Pitchers sets, which despite their stupid name have a loopy charm and some decent players; the 1987 Baseball All-Stars set, which has Nolan Ryan and Don Mattingly *and* Mark Clear; and the '87 Baseball's Exciting Stars set, which lacks Mattingly but adds an early Jose Canseco card and a mid-period Don Aase card.

As we said before, this stuff is like junk food; it should not make up the bulk of your diet. But it's all right to throw a few of these sets into your mix. And if they go up in value, so much the better.

85

Buy lesser-known tobacco cards.

T213, T208, T222 and others are not just names. In fact, they are scarce, in some cases even rare, types of tobacco cards. They are not just distant cousins, but perilously close to identical twins of the enormously popular T206s. To the uninitiated, telling some of them from T206s is impossible as the differences in some cases are merely the type of tobacco on the back, the sharpness of color on the front and the color of the printing.

Ironically, many of the other tobacco cards (after getting past the big three—T205, T206 and T207) are priced at levels similar to the much more common T206s. It doesn't make a lot of sense, except to say that the demand for a T213 is not very high as they are rather tough to find so there are few if any real collectors.

That said, we run into a perplexing situation. If there is no supply and no demand, what does that do to prices? The current answer seems to be that it prices them at about the same levels as T206s. Even if they are particularly rare, you might price them high but accept far less money. The general thinking seems to be that unless someone is specifically collecting T206s, he or she will pay about the same for a Tinker whether it's a T206 or a slightly different type.

The guess here is that this way of thinking may change with collecting patterns in the years ahead. Already some cards, such as T214s and T222s, have broken out from the pack to demand significantly higher prices than T206s and the others. Look for the trend to continue.

As people begin to collect earlier cards they find that it's not really in the price range of many to attempt a complete collection of T206s. An interesting alternative is a type collection with one of each different card made during a given period or perhaps even a Hall of Famer of each of the cards produced during a given period. Either way, that spells something of a change in the form of people actually wanting things like T213s. If that happens there's a real surprise in the wings.

T213s were made only in Louisiana, so production levels were not exactly enormous. In the case of other issues similar considerations apply. Place any demand at all on such limited supplies and you have a nearly certain price rise. This is especially true when you're talking about these lesser known tobacco issues in high grades.

While it would probably be too much to expect something like a T209, even in higher grades, to suddenly skyrocket, it does not seem all that farfetched to see prices on some of these issues climb to much better levels when compared to T206s.

86

Sell your mint cards.

You've already heard the arguments. Mint cards go up in value faster and higher than any other grade. On paper that's absolutely correct, so on paper this has to be one of the dumbest ideas since the Red Sox traded Red Ruffing for Cedric Durst and $50,000.

The problem is there's a catch. Actually there are a couple of catches. The first is whether your Mint cards actually are Mint and can bring Mint card prices. Just because a friendly dealer or other collector says a card is Mint does not make it so. In fact, by today's Mint grading standards a fair number of cards taken directly from packs would not qualify as Mint.

That is just for modern cards. In the case of a Mantle rookie, the potential buyer is likely to be even more fussy and it makes sense since with $20,000 at stake as opposed to three dollars, the buyer is likely to be much, much tougher with grading.

So the first catch in buying Mint

cards is: Can you correctly identify them and will potential buyers agree with you? The sad fact for many is that their grading skills are simply not up to the test.

The second catch is related to the first. In many other collectible markets, as prices have risen, grading standards have changed, becoming more rigid. In a way it makes sense, as in the case of the Mantle rookie as opposed to the average rookie taken straight from a pack.

Quite literally you could correctly identify and purchase a Mint card one year only to find out a few years later that no one who is a potential buyer will accept the card as Mint. Consequently the $250 Mint card you purchased, which should now be worth $1,000, due to no fault of your grading it has become a Near Mint card worth only $275. Your paper profits of $750 have evaporated into a real profit of $25!

Some people have made a lot of money with Mint cards of all sports, but most of them are dealers, and many a dealer will admit if pressed that he too has purchased cards at one grade and had to sell them at a lower grade. The odds that you'll be one of the few who will avoid both catches in the buy-Mint hype are not very good. That's why most should sell their Mint cards and buy cards of a more stable although less financially spectacular grade.

87

Donate modern commons.

Figure this one out. There are people all over this land using valuable floor, closet, bookshelf and probably even attic space to store their modern commons, and for no earthly reason.

Consider the fact that you can buy low grade commons from the early 1900s for a few dollars. Their modern counterparts are conservatively 100 times more common and have the appreciation potential of paint chips, yet there they sit waiting for the buyer who will never come.

There are two main reasons for saving commons. The first is that stars don't always surface in their first year or two. No one can dispute that point, but it's equally true that after four or five years in any league a player's potential (or lack thereof) will show. It's just simple folly to think that after a number of years Rob Nelson will be the next Lou Gehrig any more than Randy Velischek will be the next Bobby Orr. They are commons now and will always be commons and there are hundreds of players like them with no hope of Hall-of-Fame inductions. That means their cards are commons and always will be commons with no sudden Cecil Fielder price jumps in the offing.

The second reason for saving commons can be the mistaken notion that some day they too will increase in value. Realistically, any potential increase is too minimal to take seriously. Where 1948 Bowmans are concerned it might be possible, but in the post-1980 era production levels are so high and the number of cards retained is so great that future price increases will be minimal at best.

The proof can be found in the dealers. Try to take a small group of, say, 25,000 commons to virtually any dealer. Let's assume they are Mint and catalog at an average of 5¢ each. Does anyone seriously think the dealer will pay $1,250, which is what the catalog would be? If, and it's a big if, the dealer is willing to make any offer at all it's likely to be closer to $125 than $1,250. The reason is that modern commons are exactly that. There is no real demand and the supply might well stretch to Saturn and back.

Then consider the fact that the money spent purchasing them could be earning interest, plus the fact that rent and heat and other expenses of the building where they might be stored have to be paid, and you understand that sitting on piles of commons is not free.

In most cases the problem with modern commons is not getting a good price so much as getting rid of them period. Giving them away for Halloween is one option. There are many others, but the general situation remains—they simply have little or no value and even shipping them to someone willing to pay the few dollars they are worth tends to be a losing proposition thanks to shipping costs.

The problem with commons mounts each year as top rookies fail or as unopened packs and boxes accumulate, and all the time you do nothing to dispose of them the problem only becomes worse.

Perhaps the best solution is simply to find a worthy

group and donate them. You save on the cost of storing them and may even be able to take a charitable deduction. Deduction or not, ridding yourself of commons is common sense.

88

Identify Hall of Famers early.

It makes no sense whatsoever, but it happens constantly. A player like Robin Yount goes unnoticed for years until he finally reaches the 3,000-hit plateau, making him automatic at Cooperstown. As he approaches 3,000 (say at about 2,800) people suddenly discover him, start buying his card and the prices shoot up.

What is silly about all of this is that instead of buying as Yount approached the 3,000 plateau and thus paying higher prices, people could easily have bought Yount cards a few years earlier for a lot less and then watched their investments soar when Yount was discovered. The same thing happened with Carlton Fisk, whose rookie card went from about $12 to about $125 one summer, and will happen over and over in baseball and other sports.

So how do you cash in on Hall-of-Famers-to-be? The answer is simple—it's called research. If you wait until someone prints a list of likely inductees it's already too late.

The research itself is relatively easy. Start by looking for players approaching milestones in their sports. The best-known milestones are baseball's 3,000 hits or 300 wins for a pitcher. Other sports have similar milestones, be they points scored, yards rushing or goals scored. Find the number that means virtually automatic Hall-of-Fame membership and look for players in decent health still playing reasonably well who can be expected on the basis of average years to reach big milestones in five years. They are the first cards you should be buying.

Don't stop with just the obvious. All-time save leaders, interception leaders, top goalies and even managers and head coaches are worth checking and the statistics with which to do it are there waiting for you.

There are a few positions in sports where statistics tend to be misleading. Defensemen in hockey generally don't have many goals, while offensive linemen in football don't have much of anything except bruises, but that doesn't matter. Keep track of all-star teams each year and how often given players make it at certain less glamorous positions. Usually somewhere beyond seven All-Star appearances by a player and it's time to start loading up on his cards.

Remember that your goal is to get the cards of the player before he is discovered by everyone else. That means you're already too late for some of the surest Hall of Famers in sports, such as Larry Bird, Magic Johnson, Michael Jordan, Wayne Gretzky, Nolan Ryan and Joe Montana, but you know who is in the same class as a sure shot? One Anthony Munoz, possibly the greatest offensive lineman in history. His cards aren't exactly flying out of the stores right now, but they should be, and you should be the reason why.

89

Sell checklists.

Talk about hype. There are actually people out there who pay dearly for checklists. That's right, those disappointing little lists of every card from #104 to #250 or whatever. As kids we didn't even consider them cards, and that's part of the reason for their prices today.

Go back a few decades and picture a kid opening a pack of cards hoping for *Pee Wee Reese* or *Yogi Berra*. Instead, the kid is greeted by something that has no picture and no real reason for living except that it told you what cards had been printed. Any normal kids either used it to check off what cards they had or simply threw it away as a cruel trick of Topps. Some would try and use them as the first card in schoolyard flipping, but that was frowned on many places; whether a checklist was even a card was sometimes a hotly debated topic.

That debate still continues today in a way. Some, correctly pointing out that few checklists remain in top grades, are willing to pay good prices for them. To them, all cards are of equal interest as they all mean money, but to others that's missing the point.

Yes, cards can mean money, but they mean other things as well. That 1955 Topps Gil Hodges may be the closest thing you can get to that great afternoon when Hodges and Wes Westrum collided at the plate in a critical game in the Polo Grounds. That card is a card, money and nostalgia and a lot of it. The checklist, however, has no nostalgia. It was a computer printout before its time. And an unused checklist is even worse, for it was never used to trace the progress of a collection. It's an object without purpose, a pair of gloves in Miami or a snorkel in North Dakota. To many, it's not really part of a complete set, and only to a few is it a card that would be purchased for any reason other than inclusion in a set.

The support for checklist prices comes from investors and complete set collectors who include checklists. There might be Babe Ruth collectors or San Diego Padre collectors, but there are few if any checklist collectors.

It must be remembered that the ultimate consumer of cards is the collector and most collectors had no use for checklists as kids. A great increase in collector demand for checklists is about as likely as the birth of a great hue and cry among collectors for cards of garden implements. Consequently, the price future for checklists is not bright. Sell them. Put your money on real cards.

90

Sell the strange.

Answer: Eric Lindros, the San Diego Chicken and Frank Umont.

Question: Name three baseball cards having no particular reason for their existence.

It's not just baseball that has such cards, either. There were football cards featuring diagrams of plays and hockey cards showing the trophies (and not merely the Stanley Cup) awarded at the end of each year.

In fact, in light of the possibilities, at least Frank Umont (an umpire) had some vague reason for having a card, as opposed to a hockey player and a mascot, and if anything, the trend toward strange additions to regular card sets is likely to continue as companies seek any possible selling point for their cards as opposed to those of their competitors. Why they think that edge might be gained through cards of wives, mascots, children, announcers and anyone or anything else even remotely associated with the sport defies most logic.

Also at odds with logic is the fact that some people pay money for such cards. Even more perplexing is that people in many cases pay more money than they would for a common or even a potential Hall of Famer in a given sport. Some players will actually make the Hall of Fame and in 100 years they will still be remembered. Can anyone seriously suggest that the San Diego Chicken will still be remembered or that Eric Lindros will have any more business with a baseball bat than he does now?

If you can find a buyer for non-Hall of Fame umpires and officials, trophies, chickens and whatever else might lurk in your holdings, don't quibble about the price, just take the money and run.

91

Sell sportscasters.

Let's get serious. Joe Garagiola has been one of the nicest and most interesting guys involved in baseball for years. He may make "The Today Show" Hall of Fame and he's already made Cooperstown, but not as a player. His cards may always have a bit of a premium, but because he is no longer on television on a regular basis there is no reason for large premiums as the demand for Garagiola cards can hardly be expected to go up. The same can be said of Bob Uecker, who has a $150 rookie card and a host of others.

The sportscaster of today is the forgotten man or woman of tomorrow in terms of market value. Sure, while they hold down their jobs the great exposure from television can turn a "common" name into a household celebrity, thus producing the sort of premiums seen in the Uecker rookie card, but without that spot in Cooperstown as one of baseball's immortals, with each passing year after retiring, the Bob Uecker and other sportscaster cards drop closer and closer to their ultimate "common" price fate.

It's not just baseball. Every sport has its share of former players now continuing their association through the airwaves. All of these players experience some demand for their cards, but except for the legitimate Hall of Famers, that demand will last only a short time longer than their careers.

Garagiola and Uecker are special examples, as both have expanded their careers to reach an audience much greater than that they would otherwise receive for their sports activities. That spells higher premiums than would even be normally anticipated, and looking at their card prices that observation seems to hold. But that just makes their current prices all the more precarious.

There's a simple way to look at it. The fame from a television broadcast ends when the show is over, but Hall of Fame busts remain forever. Forget the sportscaster as an investment, forget any notion of getting top price for them and sell while the selling is good, which is now because they can easily find themselves out of a job and you out of your investment with the next broadcast.

92

Sell politicians.

I have nothing against politicians beyond the normal gripes. Heck, some politicians, such as Captain Tony in Key West, are even friends of mine. They are nice people, good to their children and generally mean no one any harm. It's just that plenty of people fit into that category and *they* don't have cards, or if they do, they bring no special premium, so why should cards depicting politicians who were athletes first bring special prices?

Football seems to have the best examples of this, although Jim Bunning in baseball comes to mind. But he has potentially Hall of Fame credentials and a fairly modest political position, so his premiums are hard to evaluate.

The first card in question is the 1955 Topps of Byron "Whizzer" White. Now, the card of White is a short print so it would be $20 anyway in Near Mint condition. Because Byron White happened to become a Supreme

Court Justice, it brings double that price.

Since White just retired from the Court, his political days are over. His football career ended long ago and there isn't likely to be an enormous growth in Supreme Court Justice collectors any time soon. By all rights, that means the price premium should sink to just about common price levels, as a few years from now no one will be quite sure why Byron White brings any premium at all.

Now, Jack Kemp is a more interesting situation. Kemp was a decent quarterback in the early 1960s. He was an even better politician running for president, serving in the Bush cabinet and generally doing all the things

"WHIZZER" WHITE Halfback

that politicians do quite well. Moreover, he's viewed as having a good chance to be the Republican choice to go against Clinton.

This poses a dilemma. There has never been a president who appeared on his own card as a professional athlete. Certainly if Kemp gets the Republican nomination, and more so if he's elected president, the price of his cards is going straight through the roof along with his political fortunes.

But there's a problem in the scenario. Actually, there are two; the first is the fact that it's hardly a lock that Jack Kemp will ever be president. Yes, things look good for him right now, but he didn't exactly set the political world on fire with his last campaign.

The second problem is that Jack Kemp cards are already anything but cheap. Compared to common prices (and it must be remembered Kemp is not a Hall of Famer) his cards are currently running 60 to 300 times the price of a common in the same condition. In fact, Kemp cards are well above the levels of most Hall of Famers from the period, so the question has to be, how much higher can they go and how far can they fall?

The answer to the how-much-higher question is probably in the double to triple range, although it must be remembered we're talking about something that has never happened before.

The reason to sell Kemp, though, is the down side, which has to be viewed as roughly the difference between current prices and commons. Yes, maybe for years Kemp will bring some premium, but if he goes no further in politics, owners of his card will find there just isn't a very big cabinet member premium. It's too great a risk; sell them into what's becoming a bull market.

93

Buy unique moderns.

See these Steve Yzermans? They ought to be in your collection, as they are among the very few modern cards that are legitimately rare. In some respects people might not con-

Detroit Red Wings
Steve Yzerman

sider them cards, as they were never issued and are clearly identified as prototypes not for sale.

The total number of these Yzermans produced is estimated at around 50 of each. Similar items exist in quantities ranging from a few to a few hundred and they exist in all sports and from virtually all manufacturers.

Such rarities take a variety of forms. First there are proofs of cards that were issued. Such proofs did very well in the Topps Auction some years back but have yet to find a truly solid market. Some day they may, but be wary about paying way too much for them until they do.

Far better than proofs is an assortment of cards such as the Yzermans. Such cards, produced in extremely limited quantities, were never issued but are sometimes available in the marketplace. While their prices may range from a few hundred to a few thousand dollars per card, considering their rarity such prices are modest.

While it might be too much to expect such rarities to draw the sort of prices and attention received by regular-issue cards, they are still important examples of cards that might have been and are fairly solid investments. Just be careful to ensure that they are as presented and not promo cards or similar issues produced not by the tens and hundreds but rather by the thousands and tens of thousands.

94

Hold Magic and Bird.

Larry Bird and Earvin "Magic" Johnson seem to be forever linked in many minds, and that applies here as well. From the time the two found themselves facing each other in the NCAA finals years ago, Magic and Larry Bird have been the friendly adversaries who dominated the game of basketball during the 1980s.

With the coming of Michael Jordan and others, the years of Magic and Bird were numbered. Glory in the NBA or any sport is fleeting. Even so, the records, the championships and the impact of Bird and Magic can now easily be overlooked. Lest anyone forget, the NBA was in something of a downward slide when the two arrived on the scene but has been gaining in popularity ever since.

With their retirements, Bird and Magic cards were bound to suffer some price softening. Sure, they aren't cheap, but consider what you are getting. They are no mere Hall of Famers.

No, they are certain all-time first team NBA stars who continue to be mentioned in the same breath with Jordan and Jabbar. That's pretty impressive company by any standards and it's deserved.

It's not just that fact that makes them solid buys today, though. A whole generation discovered card collecting during the 1980s. If that generation follows the

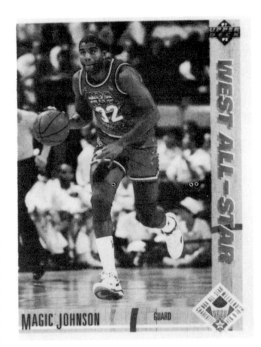

normal pattern, its members will come back to card collecting even if they leave during their teens and twenties. When they return, stars from the 1980s are likely to be their first priorities and Bird and Magic fit perfectly in that small list of the greats of the 1980s along with Joe Montana and Wayne Gretzky.

As the careers of these dominant players wane, there

will be ample opportunity and ample reason to consider a few purchases of each, but especially Bird and Magic, who truly played a major role in salvaging their sport's popularity.

No, you won't get rich with Bird and Magic, but especially in the case of their earlier cards, you're not likely to go too far wrong either.

95

Dump the junk.

Dead deer, famous clerics, tractors I've known and loved, poultry of promise—you name it and someone somewhere either has or is about to put out a card set about it.

This is not that unusual. Heaven knows, many of the first card sets of the 1880s contained billiard players, swimmers and an assortment of others from lesser sports. Heck, some of the sports such as boxing were even rivals to baseball in importance. Yet, with the exception of famous boxers, Buffalo Bill and Annie Oakley (who were famous crack shots), no one from the lesser sports brings anything like the prices even the least-known baseball players from the era command today. The reason is a simple lack of demand so pronounced that even the minimal supplies dwarf any current or even wildly imagined demand.

In light of that, what causes anyone to think that the girls of Hooters, stars of lesser TV shows and even lesser

sports figures have any particular potential? Wishful thinking, maybe. Perhaps a chemical imbalance or maybe a
lower tolerance for hype.

Yes, some of these issues are attractive enough.
Moreover, most are cheap, but so are lawn clippings and
no one saves them with an expectation of profit. The
same should be said of the minor card issues. They have
little or no potential. If you want them, that's fine, just
don't expect to make any money off them.

There may be one or two surprises in such lesser issues, such as Golden Bear or Arnold Palmer golf cards, a couple tennis greats or even NASCAR or other racing sets, but the number of such potential winners is very, very small and will in no way counterbalance the losses in all the others.

If you've got an instinct to try such sets, consider it like sticking your hand in a flame. Sure it's different—but you won't enjoy it. If you've already started with such things, stop now and get rid of what you've got because they're not going to get any better or more valuable.

Sell Deion.

Let's get this straight. Deion Sanders is a great talent, perhaps one of the best of all time. So you don't like his attitude, the private planes from one event to the next or whatever. The fact still remains, he's a great athlete and if there were a Hall of Fame just for that he'd be someone to buy, not to sell.

The problem with Deion is that with all that talent he's a little like Bo Jackson without the injury. Sure, he can play two sports and he can do them well, but so far no one born can do both at Hall-of-Fame levels.

So what happens is his card prices go fairly high because he's so widely recognized, but in the end he's headed for no Hall of Fame and his card prices are headed down. Sell now while he's famous and healthy, because if you wait too long he may not be either, much less both.

Sell basketball cards and flop the profits into baseball cards.

Basketball is hot right now. Everything basketball is hot. Basketball shirts, basketball shoes, basketball video games, basketball talk, basketball books, basketball skills, basketball players, and basketball cards—everything, in fact, except Action Packed's All-Star Gallery basketball cards, which you could have guessed. Who wants a puffy card of Dave Bing, anyhow?

Because basketball is so hot, prices are really moving up for both new and old basketball cards. If there's any segment of the overall card market that is inflated right now, it's basketball cards.

And you must have some basketball cards kicking around. Everyone does. Every card collector worth his sale dabbled in basketball cards through the '70s and early '80s. If you were a card collector back then, check your shoeboxes; you might be surprised at what you'll find.

If you do have basketball cards kicking around, turn them. Take them to a show or to a dealer and sell them. You'll likely get top dollar for them, since they're a commodity that a dealer can turn and sell with no problems. When you get your money, take it and put it into older baseball cards—good quality stuff, the Hall of Famers and such we talked about earlier. If the dealer will let you, try to work a swap. He ought to be more than happy to swap slower-moving stuff for cards that will literally fly off his shelves.

Don't get the idea from any of this that the market for basketball cards has peaked and is headed on the fast track to nowhere. That's not the case. The basketball-card market is healthy and will remain healthy for as long as people want to be like Mike and not crank like Frank, and as long as the NBA can keep producing Shaquille O'Neals. Basketball is shaping up as a world sport to rival soccer; it's easy to learn and doesn't require much to play. Basketball also has a visionary commissioner, David Stern, who has the league's economic house in order and a TV package that must make Bud Selig and the rest of the ruling junta drool—drool more than usual, that is.

Baseball has its problems, that's for sure. It has no leadership and no idea of where it's headed. The huge reservoir of goodwill it built up over the years is dwindling. Does that mean basketball cards will supplant baseball cards in popularity? Perhaps, at some point. Does that mean that people will stop collecting baseball cards in favor of basketball cards? No. Basketball is a here-and-now sport; there's little nostalgia connected with basketball. Baseball, on the other hand, is steeped in nostalgia. That's a great part of its appeal. And a portion of that nostalgia is tied up in baseball cards. People won't ever stop collecting baseball cards; they may stop collecting basketball cards. That's the one abiding reason to dump and switch.

98

Work geographically.

Our friends Jim McLauchlin and Hal Hintze have this little thing that they do. No, not that thing, silly; instead they do a little tradeout that benefits both sides and shows what you can do when you work the card market geographically. Jim works (worked, if you want to get technical) for a string of card stores in the Twin Cities; Hal lives in Wisconsin, sets up at shows occasionally, and buys a lot of cards for "research purposes." (Sure, Hal.) In the course of buying cards, Hal gets a lot of Minnesota Twins and Vikings; in the course of busting packs trying to get Vikings and Twins to sell as singles in his stores, Jim gets a lot of Packers and Brewers. So the two guys basically trade Vikings and Twins for Packers and Brewers even-up. Jim gets more singles he can sell at a profit in his stores and Hal gets cards he can make money on when he sets up. Both guys come out ahead on the deal and the world is a better place for it.

Hal also has this thing he does at shows outside of his highly concentrated hometown, Wausau, Wisconsin. He goes around the floor buying up cards of Johnny "Bear Tracks" Schmitz. Schmitz is a common everywhere but Wausau, where he's a hometown boy. Hal knows he can buy Johnny Schmitz cards for dirt anywhere but Wausau and sell them at a premium in Wausau. It's not a reason in and of itself for Hal to go to a distant show, but as long as he's there he doesn't mind doing a little something that will net him a tidy profit.

Now you're probably saying to yourself, "Yeah, but I don't set up at shows and I don't work for a string of card stores and I don't have a big-leaguer from my hometown and I don't get out of the house and that sounds like too much work and I can't dooooo that." Well, if you are, cut it out; you're whining again. The fact is that even if you're a semi-lowly collector you can make geography work for you.

Here's how.

The first thing you need to find is a semi-advanced collector like yourself who buys some cards with the thought of selling them at some future date, and lives in a region geographically removed from you. You can find such collectors through the classified ads in *Sports Collectors Digest*. Once you find this guy or guys or gal or combination thereof, you funnel him the regional stars and semi-commons that are popular in his area in exchange for the regional stars and semi-commons people in your area are clamoring for. In this way, you can work the geographic end of the market without ever leaving the comfort of your beanbag chair surrounded by the world's largest deposit of aluminum (in can form, of course).

If you're a little more ambitious and get out of the house from time to time, stop in local card stores when you're on the road and proffer your carefully chosen supply of regional stars and in-demand semi-commons in exchange for the slow-moving stuff that is fast-moving stuff back where you hail from. Sometimes the difference in value is so great you can buy from an outlying dealer and sell to a hometown dealer and still make money on the transaction.

Regional-collecting hotbeds are Detroit, Cleveland, St. Louis, Chicago, and the New York area. Cool regions of the country include the Deep South and the Southwest. If you're from Chicago and make frequent business trips to, say, Albuquerque, you can make a bit of money on cards by buying your Blackhawks and Bears down there and selling them back home.

Believe it or not, the large evil monolithic card market is actually a bunch of small, friendly card markets that you can use to your advantage. See if it ain't so.

99

Buy Tiffany sets.

Most of the pariahs of the card business are sets that peaked too soon. Take Sportflics, for instance. These ultra-thick, triple-action, extra-expensive cards hit the market in 1986, long before football cards like Action Packed and Collector's Edge, long before the advent of super-premiums like Stadium Club and Ultra. They pioneered tamper-proof packs and readable full-color card backs, and they just died. Even today you can buy Sportflics sets for less than their issue price.

And the baseball-card battleground is littered with similar cards: Topps Bigs, whose oversized cards predated Fleer GameDay by half a decade and that were scorned two of the three years of their existence; Scoremasters, which merged art and baseball long before Upper Deck ever tried anything in that area and were an even bigger dog on the market than Bigs; and Topps Tiffany sets, which promised ultra-premium, limited-edition cards at ultra-premium prices and rarely sold enough copies to pay the light bill.

Tiffany sets are UV-coated, higher-quality versions of regular Topps (and Bowman) cards that were sold as complete sets at time of issue for a hefty tariff—usually $125 or more. There's no doubt the cards were worth it, especially compared to the regular Topps cards of the day. Edition size varied wildly from 5,000 sets in 1985 and '86 and again at the very end in 1991 to roughly 30,000 in 1988 and 1989. There were also Bowman Tiffany sets in 1989 and 1990.

You can get a 1987, 1989 or 1990 Topps Tiffany set, and 1988 and '89 Bowman Tiffany sets, for less than $100—a heck of a buy, when you figure that a limited amount was made and super-premium cards are all the rage.

If our logic leaves you unimpressed, maybe a little math will help. Topps made more than 125,000 cases of some of its baseball sets in the years 1984-91. A standard case of cards consists of 20 boxes, each containing 36 packs, with 15 cards per pack. A little long multiplication tells you that there are 10,800 cards in a standard case, meaning that Topps made 1.35 billion cards in one of those years. Assuming there were 792 cards in the Topps set that given year, the total number of sets that could have been assembled from the Topps press run was 1,704,545. Now, if given a choice between one of 1.7 million for $30 or one of 28,000—and a better-looking one at that—for $89, which would you choose?

The disparity between press run and value is even more marked in Fleer's abortive run of Tiffany-type sets. The company made glossy versions of its 1987-89 sets and sold them in collectors' tins with World Series sets available nowhere else. The sets were absolutely the hottest thing going for a very short time in 1987, when no one could get them because Fleer hadn't shipped everyone quite yet, but they cooled quite rapidly when it became apparent that 125,000 had been made, and more reports of possible duplicate serial numbers drove the sets into a tailspin from which they have never recovered. The 1987 set sells for little more than the catalog value of the non-glossy version—actually less, in some ads we've seen—and the 1988 and '89 sets sell for only slightly more.

Even if there were more than 125,000 1987 Fleer glossy tins made, that's still a relatively small number. And the set is a great set full of great players; how can you go wrong by paying less for it than you would for a regular '87 Fleer set?

We're not advocates of the weird. Okay, we are advocates of the weird. But we're also advocates of value. And we just plain believe that Tiffany sets, Fleer tin glossy sets, and even the one Score glossy set produced (1988) represent great value.

100

Buy minor-league team sets.

With the collapse of the rookie-card market, about the only way collectors can make money off of younger players is by staying one step ahead of the card companies. While this led some half-baked baseball-card satirists to claim that the only thing left for the card companies to do is a set of Little League cards with an "In The Cradle" subset, the reality is that the way to stay one step ahead of the Major League Prospects subsets and their ilk is by buying the right minor-league team sets.

Minor-league team sets really are the way to go for collector/investors who spotlight certain players and follow them through the minors. The reasons: Production and distribution. Most minor-league team sets are produced in quantities of 5,000-10,000 sets— and 5,000 more often than 10,000. The two major companies that still produce team sets, Classic-Best and Fleer/ProCards, keep production down to minimize their exposure, since in most cases fewer sets sell than are printed. Also, minor-league team sets are sold only through a handful of dealers—Don Harrison's 10th Inning (3324 W. Mercury Blvd., Hampton, VA 23666) and Bill Wesslund's Portland Sports Cards (2401 N.E. Broadway St., Portland, OR 97232) being two of the biggest—and through the individual teams. You can't walk into a Wal-Mart and find a Classic-Best Harrisburg Senators set with Cliff Floyd. The only Cliff Floyd minor-league cards you can buy come in foil packs—and they're different from the team-set versions.

Minor-league team sets usually sell for around $5-$7.50 apiece their year of issue, meaning there's the potential for dropping a lot of money on the wrong minor-league team set if you buy multiples of that set (which is recommended; 'tis better to roll the dice and cast your lot with a handful of players than buy a set from here and a set from there). Production values aren't the greatest with minor-league team sets, either. Perhaps the worst baseball card ever made shows the Omaha Royals' Kevin Seitzer taken from a vantage point somewhere in Nebraska, but somewhere closer to North Platte than Omaha. And then there's Kit Kiefer's favorite, the Classic-Best team-set card of Marc Kubicki showing Kubicki's ID picture (the picture taken by the photograher with the player holding his name up, written on a slate, so the photographer can identify the player after he takes the real picture), but spelling the poor guy's name "Marc Kubiki" on the card.

So? Production values aren't a big deal with these cards, foil-pack or team-set version. The important thing is finding the right player or group of players to go after. Multiples are nice. Some of the best minor-league team sets of the past several years have been the 1987 Gastonia Rangers, with Juan Gonzalez, Dean Palmer and Sammy Sosa; the '89 Best Jacksonville Expos, with Delino DeShields and Marquis Grissom; and the '93 Fleer and Classic-Best Greenville Braves, with Mike Kelly, Chipper Jones, Javy Lopez, and Tony Tarasco.

Minor-league team sets are a gamble that can tie up

your money, no doubt about it. But buy cheap in the year of issue, look for multiple-star teams, don't expect instant results and you stand a very good chance of coming out ahead.

Buy minor-league cards the year they're issued, because everyone wants them the year after.

Oh, it's hell being a minor-league cardmaker. Talk to the people who make minor-league cards, big companies who make enough money making big-league cards to buy themselves corporate jets and big corporate castles with corporate alligators swimming in the corporate moats and corporate coral atolls and corporate Central American republics, and they complain about how hard it is to make money on minor-league cards because no one buys minor-league cards the year they're issued because the names of the players look like this to them:

Mike "Spats" OoooOOgala&&$#@@@!!!oo&^^RFRrr#gachuckkka.

And they can't remember that.

Instead, most of the people who buy minor-league cards buy them the year after they're released, when the prospects and the suspects sort themselves out more and a few of the players are even on major-league rosters and no longer have to put up with minor-league indignities like sleeping in Holiday Inns and eating at Burger King. Major-leaguers get to stay at luxury hotels and eat at fine restaurants, though if you ask them the difference between staying at Holiday Inns and eating at Burger Kings versus staying at luxury hotels and eating in fine restaurants, you're apt to get an answer something like this:

"EEEeeuuuuurrrrppppppppCHHH!!!"

And an M-80 down your pants.

All of this, as you might guess, has dire consequences for the large card company, because no one wants to buy minor-league cards the year they're issued but instead wants to wait until that precise moment when the cards hit "the secondary market" to do his or her buying, leaving the cardmaker cut out of the profit picture and unable to make the payments on its corporate planet of the solar system.

The "secondary market" is the one where the people who make the money are not monolithic card companies but entrepreneurial small businesspeople who can also sell you Rolex watches and Gucci bags as well as things you once owned but didn't know you didn't anymore.

NO! Actually, dealers embody the ideals of the American way, namely: honesty, fairness, reverence, misleading advertising and ruthless price-slashing. They make their money on minor-league cards by being the only people buying the cards when they're originally offered, and then turning around and selling the cards to collectors who want the cards at highly inflated (but honestly, reverently fair) prices as soon as a few names emerge from the murk.

There's no reason you can't get in on this yourself. When minor-league foil packs are first advertised in the trading-card periodicals, buy several boxes. Hang onto them for a minimum of a year, then take them to shows—ideally as part of your own table setup—and sell them. By that time the price for foil boxes should have gone up enough for you to make a nice profit on the transaction, pleasing you to no end and swiping another dollar or two from the pockets of the monolithic card entities.

Minor-league cards are a curious part of the larger and more curious trading-card market. They present a lot of opportunity and only a little peril. All they require is that you change around your timing a little. And for a few extra bucks, you can do that—can't you?

Bonus Books for the Serious Collector

Collecting Baseball, Basketball, Football, Hockey Cards
Experts tell where to find hidden value
Paul M. Green and Tony Galovich
ISBN 0-929387-84-8
224 pages—$8.95—paper

Making Money with Baseball Cards
A handbook of insider strategies
Paul M. Green and Donn Pearlman
ISBN 0-933893-77-9
215 pages—$7.95—paper

Collecting Baseball Cards—Third Edition
All-time bestseller
Donn Pearlman
ISBN 0-929387-20-1
123 pages—$7.95 paper

The Top 100
The best baseball cards to own, ranked and rated for the investor and collector
Paul M. Green and Kit Kiefer
ISBN 0-933893-88-4
303 pages—$8.95—paper

Collecting Football Cards for Fun and Profit
How to buy, store, and trade them
Chuck Bennett with Don Butler
ISBN 0-929387-32-5
158 pages—$8.95—paper

Collecting Sports Autographs
Fun and profit from this easy-to-learn hobby
Tom Owens
ISBN 0-933893-79-5
131 pages—$6.95—paper

Bonus Books, Inc., 160 East Illinois Street, Chicago, Illinois 60611

TOLL-FREE: 800 • 225 • 3775 **FAX: 312 • 467 • 9271**